Eco-Tech

Sustainable Architecture and High Technology

Eco-Tech

Sustainable Architecture and High Technology

Catherine Slessor

Photographs by John Linden

With 356 illustrations, 112 in colour

Thames and Hudson

Title page The atrium at Channel Four Headquarters by Richard Rogers Partnership (page 104).

© 1997 Thames and Hudson Ltd, London
Text © 1997 Catherine Slessor
Photographs © 1997 John Linden

British Library Cataloguing-in-Publication Data
A catalogue record for this book is available from the British Library

ISBN 0-500-34157-5

Printed and bound in Singapore by C. S. Graphics

Contents

Introduction

The expression of technological achievement has been a key concern in the development of modern architecture. Early Modernists such as Le Corbusier and Gropius regarded technology as a transforming force for change, and therefore one that should be appropriated and celebrated in a truly modern architecture. From Peter Behren's 1909 turbine hall for AEG in Berlin through to Mies van der Rohe's 1958 Seagram Building, modern architecture has consistently affirmed and alluded to the notion of technological progress. Most recently – and perhaps most explicitly – this sensibility has been reflected in the evolution of High-Tech architecture, a movement that has its origins in the technologically optimistic 1960s. This was the era that saw the aerospace industry put men on the moon and the plug-in provocations of the Archigram group raise the consciousness of an entire generation of architects, including such current influential practitioners as Richard Rogers, Nicholas Grimshaw and Michael Hopkins.

A critical aspect of the interaction between architecture and technology is the way in which they have continually redefined each other. High-Tech has moved on from an early preoccupation with the arid logic of mass production wedded to extreme functionalism. What began as the introduction of rationalized industrial processes into building construction to create neutral, flexible, expendable, environments has evolved into an increasingly diffuse and complex style. This sensibility now embraces wider concerns, including place-making, social responsiveness, energy use, urbanism and ecological awareness, 'Eco Tech' as opposed to High Tech. Instead of being unthinkingly glorified, technology is more selectively exploited to achieve particular ends. Examples of this might include a structural system based on and engineered to resemble a giant organic ribcage or a translucent cladding panel that has a high level of insulation, or an environmental control system that can forecast the demands of building users and respond accordingly.

Crucial to this selective approach is the creative interaction of many previously semi-interdependent disciplines – for instance, structural and services engineering, materials, computer and ecological sciences – resulting in architecture that offers a much wider variety of experience never possible before and that can adapt to the changing needs of contemporary society. Richard Rogers, one of architecture's most articulate and visionary practitioners, argues that 'The creation of an architecture which incorporates new technologies entails breaking away from the platonic idea of a static world, expressed by the perfect finite object to which nothing can be added or taken away, a concept which has dominated architecture since its beginning. Instead of Schelling's description of architecture as frozen music we are looking at an architecture more like some modern music, jazz or poetry, where improvisation plays a part,

The interior of the British Pavilion, designed for the 1992 Seville Expo by Nicholas Grimshaw and Partners (page 88). The lightweight temporary building combined a range of ingenious climate-modifying features – such as a cooling water-wall powered by solar panels – but more importantly, showed that High-Tech architecture and environmental responsiveness need not be mutually exclusive.

The vast Glass Hall, by Ian Ritchie in collaboration with Von Gerkan Marg and Partners, at Leipzig's trade fair site (page 68). A contemporary reinterpretation of the nineteenth-century Crystal Palace archetype, it exploits modern building technologies to achieve structural elegance and an extraordinary level of transparency.

an indeterminate architecture containing both permanence and transformation.'[1]

This book explores the technological, social and architectural concerns that inform Eco-Tech architecture. The extraordinarily diverse range of buildings presented in the six sections – Structural Expression, Sculpting with Light, Energy Matters, Urban Responses, Making Connections, Civic Symbolism – illustrate an equally extraordinary range of forms and functions. Inevitably, some projects share more than one defining characteristic, yet all consistently display an almost unbounded degree of optimism about the way architecture and technology can learn from each other.

Structural Expression

The great structural engineer Ove Arup once remarked, 'What the engineer sees as a structure, the architect sees as a sculpture. Actually, of course, it is both.' The increasing potential of expression through structural engineering is an obvious embodiment of the symbiosis between architecture and technology. As interpreters and proponents of technological possibilities, engineers have progressively broadened their role from unseen, unsung functionaries to active collaborators working in creative coalition with architects. With the growth of such multidisciplinary engineering practices as Ove Arup & Partners, a new generation of architect-engineer has begun to achieve prominence. Until his death in 1992, Peter Rice brilliantly exemplified this hybrid philosophy, although he was gently dismissive of the label, citing the engineer's need to approach design problems objectively. Yet Rice also had a strong streak of romanticism – Jonathan Glancey described him as the 'James Joyce of engineering' – that enabled him to confound received wisdom and turn accepted rules of building on their head.

One of the century's most influential and poetically expressive engineers, Rice originally worked on the Sydney Opera House, as part of Ove Arup's team, and later on a succession of major buildings that included Paris's Pompidou Centre (1977) and the Lloyd's Building in London (1986), both notable for their innovative exposed structures. More recently he was involved with the Stansted and Kansai airports (pages 158 and 130), two projects that spectacularly evoke the drama of flight, and the wave-like TGV station in Lille (page 154). Throughout his career Rice believed that the true role of the engineer was to explore the potential of materials and structures in the manner of the medieval masons and the pioneering Victorians, whose soaring stone cathedrals and cast-iron structures still reflect the physical feel of the materials with which they were made as well as the character of those who built them – what he called the *traces de la main*.

Santiago Calatrava is another architect-engineer who is exploring the limits of structural expression. Synthesizing sculptural, architectural and engineering skills, Calatrava has produced an iconoclastic series of bridges and buildings in Europe that challenge mainstream practice. With the Alamillo Bridge in Seville, for example (page 34), the basic laws of engineering mechanics are used as a springboard for formal expression, and the result is a piece of abstract sculpture that draws on both Gothic and modern cable-stayed structural principles. More recently, as in the Trinity Bridge in Salford (page 36), Calatrava has been experimenting with lightweight materials and the aesthetics of structural and visual tension.

The engineering tradition in architecture dates back to the industrial architects of the nineteenth century, such as Joseph Paxton, Gustave Eiffel and Isambard Kingdom Brunel. Their innovative yet functional structures were made possible through newly discovered technologies of prefabrication. The invention of cast iron, for example, suggested new ways of building and understanding structure that were wholly different from existing masonry construction. The archetypal building of this period was Joseph Paxton's Crystal Palace, a colossal glass hall built to house the Great Exhibition of 1851. Both structurally and typologically, the Crystal Palace is regarded as an enduring example of technology pushed to the limit. It is perhaps the first genuinely High-Tech building and a continuing source of inspiration for contemporary architects, particularly in its iconic expression of structure and materials. Ian Ritchie's barrel-vaulted Glass Hall in Leipzig (page 68), designed in collaboration with Von Gerkan Marg and Partners, is a late-twentieth-century version of the Crystal Palace that uses modern structural and material technologies of trussed steel arches and silicone-jointed glass sheets held in place by cast-steel finger fixings.

Advances in structural technology are not only evident in the physical achievements of these spectacular buildings but in the design process that created them. The advancement of computer-aided-design (CAD) software and ever more powerful computers have enabled engineers and architects to create structures of unprecedented complexity. Sophisticated computer models of intricate geometries are now an integral part

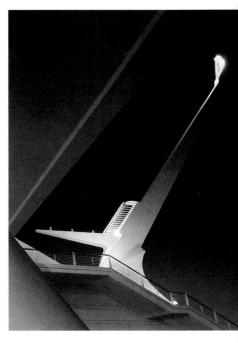

The approach to the Alamillo Bridge in Seville by Santiago Calatrava (page 34) dramatizes the structure's sculptural quality.

Inspired by natural forms and brought into being by computer simulation and analysis, the steel-lattice shells of the Museum of Fruit at Yamanashi by Itsuko Hasegawa (page 46) are a poetic fusion of nature and technology.

of the mathematical process needed to analyze a building's structural behaviour. The increased power to investigate and assess a broader and more involved range of forms has led to enormous advances. It would have been impossible to build the tensile fabric roof of the Inland Revenue staff complex (page 98) twenty years ago, or the steel lattice shells of the Museum of Fruit (page 46), because the computation required to analyze – much less create – their geometry would have been too laborious to execute.

The computer's potential to reveal new concepts of form and order in the natural world has also begun to exert an influence on architectural design. Many natural structures, such as spiders' webs and soap bubbles, generate their own organic forms and could therefore not be assessed by using conventional mathematical models. While small versions of such forms are relatively easy to make, it has only recently become possible to create large-scale versions for use in buildings. During the late 1950s, the German engineer Frei Otto began experimenting with calculations of structural behaviour extrapolated from small models, but the real breakthrough happened when computers became powerful and sophisticated enough to simulate the process of a structure finding its own form.

Using computer simulation, many contemporary architects, such as Renzo Piano, are exploring and drawing inspiration from natural forms. The distinctly

organic appearance of Kansai Airport (page 130) represents a marked evolution from the mechanical, kit-of-parts style of Piano's earlier projects, such as the Pompidou Centre. Kansai consummately displays Piano's extensive research into building technologies that match the efficiency of nature, insights made possible by advances in mathematics and computing. Yet for all this, architects and engineers still have some catching up to do; it is perhaps salutary to consider that a single orchid contains more variety and subtlety of structural actions than the most remarkable building.

Sculpting with Light

Since the technical and commercial development of large-scale glass envelopes during the second half of the nineteenth century, the notion of transparency has exerted a seductive hold on the architectural imagination. Le Corbusier's canonical description of architecture as 'the masterly, correct and magnificent play of masses brought together in light' affirmed a new set of values for modern buildings – transparency and dematerialization achieved through material lightness and spatial interpenetration. The poetic and technical potential of transparency was perhaps most famously epitomized by Pierre Chareau and Bernard Bijvoët's Maison de Verre in Paris, with its main external wall constructed from translucent glass lenses. Since then, the increasing sophistication of glass and lightweight transparent

plastics has presented architects with new and richer possibilities. Jean Nouvel, whose work strives to encapsulate the 'airy poetry of evanescence', is among numerous contemporary architects pursuing these themes. His Cartier Foundation, also in Paris (page 66), is a series of exquisitely transparent planes set in a mature garden, the building mass dissolving in a mesmeric play of light and reflection.

In the last twenty years, the art and science of transparency has been pushed to new boundaries, particularly by High-Tech architects eager to exploit new cladding materials and fixing technologies with the same pioneering zeal as their predecessors of the 1920s and 1930s. The seamless reflecting skin of Norman Foster's seminal Willis Faber & Dumas building (1975), for example, has a clear historical antecedent in Mies van der Rohe's 1922 project for a glass tower, with a massive

meandering glass wall that was intended to exploit the possibilities of inter-reflection and the changing angles of light. With its specially developed curtain-walling system of large glass panels hung from the top of the building and the entire assembly stiffened by glass fins, the Willis Faber structure marked a defining moment in the obsessive architectural pursuit of the uninterrupted transparent surface.

More recently, architects, engineers and manu-facturers have developed even more minimal ways of configuring glass walls and roofs, notably in hanging glazed panels from point fixings. The synergy of a steel structure combined with the tensile properties of glass has greatly advanced contemporary ideals of lightness and transparency. At the Western Morning News Headquarters, designed by Nicholas Grimshaw & Partners (page 22), the stunning transparency of its outwardly

The luminous, crystalline form of Helmut Richter's secondary school in a Viennese suburb (page 58) is a crisply honed exercise in seamlessness and transparency.

The all-glass structure of the Museum of Glass, Kingswinford, by Design Antenna (page 62) exploits the properties of glass in compression. Although still at the prototype stage, the use of 'structural' glass has fascinating potential.

curving walls is achieved through glass panels supported at each corner by four pronged nodal connectors.

By exploiting its properties in compression, some architects have taken the notion of structural glass a stage further and developed a glass column and glass beam arrangement, giving rise to the tantalizing possibility of a completely transparent enclosure. As Michael Wigginton notes, 'It may seem perverse to use glass for functions which are more happily carried out by materials with more structural predictability, but the goal of transparency and Buckminster Fuller's "ephemeralization" have proved a great spur. It is a simple step from the use of a glass fin as a bracing device to its use as a column.'[2] Early stages of this development are manifest projects like the all-glass pavilion at the Museum of Glass (page 62) designed by Design Antenna and engineered by Dewhurst Macfarlane. Despite its relatively small scale, it represents an intriguing new direction, not only in the technical evolution of glass, but also in architecture's quest for transparency.

Energy Matters

Over the last thirty years, humankind's relationship to the natural world has come under uncomfortable scrutiny as a result of the anticipation and experience of a growing range of environmental crises. At the macro level, issues of sustainable development, energy use and environmentalism are now being addressed by most governments; on the personal scale, individual environmental consciousness has given rise to green consumerism and alternative lifestyles. Political, economical and social pressures have so far tended to determine future strategies, yet the interaction of the man-made environment with the natural world has become a profound cause for concern.

About half the energy consumed in Europe is used to run buildings and another 25 per cent is expended in transportation. This energy is mostly generated by diminishing non-renewable fossil fuels that will not be available to succeeding generations. Furthermore, the emissions produced by the conversion of these fossil fuels into energy have a proven deleterious effect on the environment. While these facts may be common knowledge, they are worth restating if only to emphasize our increasingly precarious tenure on the planet. Since the oil crisis of the early 1970s precipitated an 'exogenous shock' to the Western economy, green idealism and architecture have been fitful bedfellows. The liaison has produced various bizarre and experimental prodigy (so-called 'museli architecture'), but, as Martin Pawley has observed, the events of these years 'produced no massive lifestyle changes and, in architecture at least, no design revolution'. Twenty years later, architects are still contriving to graft air-conditioned glass stumps on to city centres from Dallas to Dacca, and most inhabitants of the First World continue to pursue disparate work, shopping and leisure activities by car.

Paradoxically, most people of the First World are dimly aware that short-term expediency must be replaced by more sustainable patterns of living, but at present very few are prepared to depart from their wasteful habits. To a great extent, this is due to a lack of fully developed, credible alternatives; moreover, the promulgation of concepts of sustainability (for everything from shopping bags to cities) is still dismayingly contingent on the lumbering and self-interested forces of politics and business.

Yet there have been numerous positive advances. These are perhaps not so evident in the physical form of architecture, but in its attendant technologies, whether in the development of new materials and products, or in the use of traditional materials in different ways, such as exploiting the thermal mass of masonry construction, for example. Slowly, agendas are changing. To this end, Brenda and Robert Vale observe, 'As car design has moved from a concern with surface styling to a concentrated effort to improve engineering performance, so architecture needs to be similarly distanced from its current concern of appearance only. It is time to stop putting the fins on the Cadillac.'[3] In his Reith Lectures of 1995, Richard Rogers propounded the view that current and future technological developments could assist in redressing the problems created by the cruder effects of industrialization. As part of a slow but gradual greening

of architecture, this already encompasses more stringent thermal performance standards, eco-labelling schemes (of building materials and products, particularly in Germany and Canada), green audits for the entire design and building process, and increasingly responsive monitoring of the energy performance of buildings once in use. In addition, new ranges of products and systems have been developed for the outer skins of buildings: translucent insulation, photovoltaic cells, improved shading and daylight-deflection systems, new types of glass and new methods of façade construction. The concept of an external skin with multiple environmental functions is not in itself new: Le Corbusier first attempted to devise a *mur neutralisant* in the early

Detail of the Exhibition Hall in Hanover (page 84) by Thomas Herzog, which combines a bold structural form with energy-saving control systems. An increased level of green awareness is giving rise to a new kind of architecture that makes inventive yet responsible use of cladding technologies and environmental control strategies.

The Cité Internationale by Renzo Piano (page 76) is an ambitious urban development that aims to distil the diversity and vitality of the city. It also explores the principle of a *mur neutralisant* – a layered, environmentally responsive wall intended to improve the energy efficiency of the buildings that make up the scheme.

1930s, for the Cité de la Refuge in Paris. Over sixty years later, Norman Foster has achieved a modern, high-performance version of a *mur neutralisant* for his complex of buildings at the science and business park in Duisburg (page 92). There, the seamless skin of the Business Promotion Centre is an environmentally engineered wall that regulates the transmission of light and heat, prevents the build-up of condensation and provides an acoustic barrier. At the Cité Internationale in Lyons (page 76) Renzo Piano also explores the principle of a layered, environmentally responsive wall to improve energy efficiency while allowing the building's occupants contact with external conditions. A shimmering outer skin of glazing intercepts the force of wind and rain, so that the conventional windows behind can remain open. In summer, the buildings can be naturally ventilated, and in winter, the

glass traps heat behind it, acting like another layer of insulation. In contrast to the lightweight materiality and technical refinement of the *mur neutralisant*, another current approach exploits the inherent thermal mass of a building as part of the environmental control strategy. Michael Hopkins and Partners' Inland Revenue Headquarters at Nottingham (page 98) is a recent notable example of this principle innovatively applied to a large-scale office complex.

In the search for a more holistic approach to design, it is clear that architecture is part of a much wider and more complex debate. Architects and engineers can develop tentative prototypes and suggest alternative solutions, but the scale and effectiveness of such achievements will invariably be influenced by broader social, political and economic concerns. Moreover, it would be simplistic to conclude that technology has all the answers; the benefits of technical advances are essentially nullified unless applied in a socially beneficial manner. As philosopher Michel Foucault once remarked, 'Technology must be social before it is technical.' Architects, engineers, planners and politicians are slowly learning to strike the difficult balance between present needs and future responsibilities.

Urban Responses

Cities are dependent for their survival on a complex interaction of systems for living, working and playing crystallized into built forms. Yet many modern cities are in crisis, overwhelmed by the alienating effects of zoning, the demise of public transport, the growth of suburban sprawl and the physical and environmental damage caused by the car. Building in the city is one of the most intractable problems facing contemporary architects, and it is exacerbated by powerful vested interests, political conflict and polemical confusion. At the heart of this dilemma is the realization that the quality of urban life is affected by a messy but vital network that has been frequently ignored by planners and traffic engineers in their attempts to divide human needs into crude, industrially attainable norms. There are, however, signs that the reductivist legacy of twentieth-century planning orthodoxies is at last on the wane. It is now possible to conceive of a more humanly rich texture of development capable of promoting strong and varied expressions of city life. Set against the homogenizing tendencies of planning and big business is the recognition of the need to re-animate the city to provide a backdrop for its essential rhythms and dramas. Such an architecture can emerge if contemporary technology is sensibly appropriated to serve public needs.

To Richard Rogers, for example, urban planning is an open and interactive framework, capable of accommodating a highly differentiated mixture of uses and events, just as the Pompidou Centre was the 'exploration of the idea of a flexible institution [as well as]

an exploration of flexible and fragmented form'. Rogers's commitment to the social and public dimension of architecture is reflected in an ongoing series of proposals for the restructuring of public space in London. Through this and other studies – including a master plan for Shanghai based on satellite neighbourhoods – Rogers has attempted to evolve a political and architectural blueprint for a new vision of the city that is both humanist and sustainable. Elsewhere, individual projects, such as the new headquarters for Channel 4 (page 104), emphasize the place-making qualities of architecture, and its ability to counteract the general dreariness and disorientation of modern cities.

Another important development in public architecture arises from the understanding that modernity and tradition need not be mutually exclusive. In Genoa, for example, Renzo Piano's strategy for recolonizing and revitalizing the city's old harbour (page 120) combines sensitive restoration and reuse of existing warehouses with a series of new elements designed in the same muscular, maritime spirit of the existing port buildings. Piano's sensitive scheme responds to this urban fabric by combining contemporary technology in traditional contexts. Likewise, in Nîmes, on a site adjacent to the Maison Carrée, one of the best-preserved Roman temples in the world, Norman Foster's design for a *médiathèque* (page 116) is a contemporary abstraction underscored by an invigorating tension between ancient and modern.

Channel 4 Headquarters by Richard Rogers Partnership (page 104) enlivens a dreary part of London through the drama of its architecture and by the way in which it responds generously and positively to the public realm.

Above Detail of the glazed vault at Waterloo International Terminal, London, by Nicholas Grimshaw and Partners (page 136). The station is a modern rendition of the nineteenth-century train shed, but in terms of passenger processing, is based on the airport model.

Opposite The swooping roof of Kansai Airport by Renzo Piano Building Workshop (page 130), A poetic fusion of the biological with the mechanical.

The key to the success of these projects is diversity. Successful cities are those that encourage heterogeneity and the interaction of functions, typologies and activities, and in so doing enhance the lives of ordinary citizens .

Making Connections

A particular kind of public statement is made by a city's nodes of transportation. From the earliest railway stations to the recent Kansai airport, buildings for transport have acted as gateways in and out of cities, as well as benchmarks of technological and social progress. Mass transport has its origins in the great pioneering railway era of the mid-nineteenth century, when the newly evolved technologies of cast and wrought iron were combined with modular glazing to conceive the typology of the train shed. The lofty long-span vaults of early London stations such as Paddington, St Pancras and Kings Cross not only efficiently dissipated the smoke and steam of the trains, but were also dramatic spaces animated by light and the muscular rhythm of repeated structure.

The metal-and-glass train shed has become an enduring archetype and one that has found increasingly sophisticated expression as railway architecture enters a new age of high-speed trains, improved networks and modern stations. Across Europe rail transport is being actively encouraged as a more sustainable alternative

to road travel on practical, economic and ecological grounds. The construction of the Channel Tunnel, an engineering feat to rival those of the Victorians, has also acted as a crucial catalyst in the development of a high-speed European rail system. Two major new stations have been built to serve it – at Waterloo in London and Lille in northern France – both spectacular reinterpretations of the glass train shed using contemporary technology and circulation management. The International Terminal at Waterloo (page 136), designed by Nicholas Grimshaw and Partners, takes the form of a great glazed, biomorphic funnel that gently curves in two directions in response to a particularly awkward site. At Lille (page 154), architect Jean-Marie Duthilleul, working with engineer Peter Rice, has turned the conventional station vault into 'fine lace floating above the train'.

Despite Waterloo's technical and formal affinity with the nineteenth-century station, its planning, organization and passenger processing strategies are based on the airport model. One of the few purely twentieth-century building typologies, the airport has evolved with startling rapidity since Heathrow began life as a huddle of tents on the western edge of London just after the Second World War. Now at the end of the century in which people learned to fly, airports are coming of age as a contemporary building type that not only has its own rationale, technology and organizational structure, but also celebrates the drama of air travel. Stansted Airport

(page 158), designed by Foster and Partners, is one of the first of this new generation. Compact and civilized, it is far removed from the physical and experiential chaos that afflicts so many modern airports, distilling a Zen-like refinement from an enormously complex brief and sharing with nineteenth-century railway stations the notion of a clearly articulated progression enveloped by a billowing, translucent roof. Another recently completed airport that attains new levels of spatial and technological sophistication is Kansai in Osaka Bay (page 130), designed by Renzo Piano. It achieves the evocative ideal of fusing the biological with the mechanical, a notion that has persisted since the beginnings of Modernism. Piano's ongoing investigations into how technology can be reconciled with nature seeks to engage the two forces in a harmonious coexistence, and many of his current projects reflect an organic integrity of form and function. At Kansai the outcome is a graceful unity of space, structure and skin that embodies a breathtaking architectural vision for the future.

Civic Symbolism

The role of buildings as public symbols has been revived in recent years. Historically, monumental buildings such as town halls, law courts or libraries represented statements of municipal confidence and optimism. Now these expressions might take different forms and seek to reflect new values, such as technological progress, civic renewal or the processes of justice. Moreover, the re-emergence of the city-state in Europe (along with attendant inter-city rivalry) has been a strong motivating factor in recent civic, cultural and infrastructural development.

In France, for example, a programme of decentralization that devolves political and economic power to the regions has enabled cities to assert their identities through vigorous plans of cultural building. The ambitious cultural and architectural remit of the Carré d'art in Nîmes (page 116) aims to establish it as the 'Pompidou Centre of the South'. Drawing together a range of activities — library, art gallery, archives, offices and restaurant — it offers space for contemporary artistic creation as well as reading, consulting, documentation and book-lending. In an another French city, Marseilles, Will Alsop's competition-winning scheme for a regional government centre (page 164) combines civic grandeur with political symbolism in a bold interplay of form and technology.

Often, it is not municipal functions but major public events that are the catalysts for civic revitalization. Galvanized by hosting Expo '92 and the Olympic Games, respectively, the cities of Seville and Barcelona instigated major development programmes during the early 1990s. Barcelona, in particular, provided a paradigm of how a formerly industrial city could transform itself into a

modern metropolis without sacrificing its pungent regional Catalan character. As Peter Buchanan noted, 'The privilege of hosting the Olympics was sought not just as something in itself, but for the huge shove it gave to the synergistically snowballing momentum needed to regenerate the city so quickly and thoroughly.'[4] Presiding over the transformed city, on the Tibidabo ridge to the north, is the Collserola communications tower (page 172) designed by Foster & Partners.

Some measure of how High Tech has diffused and evolved from its 'sheds in fields' beginnings may be gauged by Richard Rogers's European Court of Human Rights in Strasbourg (page 178), a civic building that transcends national boundaries. There, literal and metaphorical transparency, structural ingenuity and energy consciousness are synthesized into a dignified yet accessible expression of the law's role in modern European society. The building works on many levels – it is organizationally efficient, spatially dramatic, technologically appropriate and institutionally imposing. It gently alludes to the past – to Erich Mendelsohn's sinuous, organic Expressionism and the Russian Constructivism of the Vesnin brothers – yet it is incontrovertibly of its time.

The reconciliation of technological imperatives and opportunities with wider human and environmental concerns is one of the most challenging creative problems facing architecture. Describing the relationship between architecture and technology, Richard Rogers has written, 'Today, technology destabilizes and transforms the modern age … Caught in this endless upheaval, technology can be used to positive ends – to advance social justice – one of modernity's greatest ideals. Perhaps we can say that when technology is used to secure the fundamentally modern principles of universal human rights – shelter, food health care, education and freedom.'[5]

Enlightened exploitation of technological and material resources may be at the heart of the Modernist tradition, but it is clear that the notion of a Machine Age rationalism based on industrialization has undergone a profound change: the silicone chip has replaced the valve, and the 'invisible' advances of the digital era have given rise to new discoveries and insights – at the very least into the complexity and diversity of nature and the cosmos. What began as the exuberant and uncomplicated celebration of the 'poetry of equipment' has evolved into a highly refined architecture that addresses a broad spectrum of ecological and cultural issues, and suggests ways to enhance public and private life on the planet. As we strive towards an understanding of our basic needs, Eco-Tech architecture expresses the importance of a responsive symbiosis between tradition and technology, the local and the universal, nature and building.

Notes

1. Richard Rogers, *Architecture, a Modern View*, London: Thames and Hudson, 1990, page 46.
2. Michael Wigginton, *Glass in Architecture*, London: Phaidon, 1996, page 104.
3. Brenda and Robert Vale, *Green Architecture*, London: Thames & Hudson, 1996, page 14.
4. Peter Buchanan, 'Barcelona a city regenerated', *The Architectural Review*, August 1992, page 12.
5. Richard Burdett (ed), *Richard Rogers Partnership, Works and Projects*, New York: The Monacelli Press, 1996, page 8.

Structural Expression

Entrance canopy and barrel-vaulted structure
of the Exhibition Hall in Linz by Thomas Herzog
(page 38)

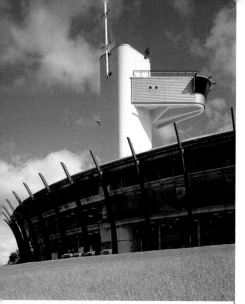

Western Morning News Headquarters

- Nicholas Grimshaw and Partners
- Plymouth, England
- 1993

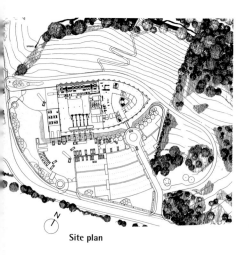

Site plan

Top The massive curving flank of the transparent external wall resembles the hull of a ship. Nautical imagery is reinforced by the boardroom 'bridge' hovering above the roof.

Above Site plan. As business expands, the building can be extended westwards, increasing the size of the machine hall and the capacity of the presses.

Opposite Detail of one of the steel 'tusks' that form part of the intricate skeletal structure of the curving wall. The weight of the suspended glass panels is transmitted to the top of the tusks by a network of stainless-steel rods and from there stresses are conveyed to the foundations.

The recent demands of technology and colour printing have had a convulsive effect on the newspaper industry. The opulent publishing fortresses of Fleet Street are now long deserted (like Bracken House, page 108), their occupants transplanted to anonymous offices or dingy sheds in the suburbs. The migration from the city centre has been repeated all over Britain, not least in Plymouth, where in 1990 the company that publishes the region's main newspaper, the *Western Morning News*, decided to relocate its operations to an edge-of-town site. Instead of opting for a standard, off-the-peg architectural solution, however, the company chose Nicholas Grimshaw and Partners, the creators of the highly acclaimed Financial Times Print Works (1988), to custom design its new headquarters.

The site is on a bluff near the airport, with entrancing views across the city towards Plymouth Sound (from where Drake set off to engage the Spanish Armada) and over the barren landscape of Dartmoor. Both the site and the client have a civic prominence: two of the company's seven newspapers (*Western Morning News* and the *Evening Herald*) have achieved a high regional profile and are regarded with strong propriatorial affection by the local populace. Unlike the brief for the Financial Times Print Works, which was essentially an elegant enclosure for machinery, here Grimshaw had to combine the below-stairs printing operations with editorial, advertising and social facilities for some 250 employees.

The building embodies the traditional model of newspaper publishing as an imperiously self-contained fiefdom, expressing both corporate and regional identity. Plymouth is a naval city, and the building's wildly romantic celebration of nautical imagery takes the form of a vast glass ship, its prow angled towards Dartmoor, sailing symbolically into the hinterland. This literal and metaphorical flagship lies cradled in a kind of dry dock hewn out of the hill, its concave glazed walls hung from massive tusk-like supports that recall the rigs that hold a vessel in place prior to the moment of launching. The organic intricacy of the glazing system, evolved from the Financial Times building, resembles a translucent bat's wing stretched tautly over slender bones, a favourite Grimshaw image magically brought into being. Hovering over the building is a pod mounted on a tower: seemingly modelled on a ship's bridge or submarine conning tower, this eyrie contains the boardroom.

The building's operations are split between a triangular prow section, given over to white-collar functions (editorial, advertising, accounts), and a huge, roughly square hall housing the printing plant. As at the Financial Times, the printing presses are exposed to the outside world in all their heroic, industrial complexity, pulsating like a ship's engine room. Reinforcing the nautical theme, a gangplank docks into the building's eastern flank, bringing visitors into a triangular atrium at the heart of the prow section.

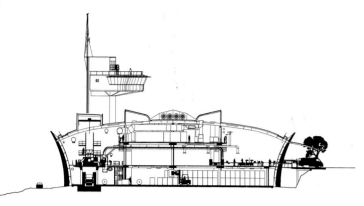

South-north cross section through machine hall and despatch

1 Atrium
2 Escape tower
3 Cellular offices
4 Reception
5 Entrance bridge
6 Entrance
7 Editorial offices
8 Plate making
9 Interim composing room
10 Photographic
11 Mechanical publishing and inserting
12 Van loading
13 Articulated vehicle loading

Top left Cross section. The building is set into the hill; a bridge brings visitors into the middle entrance level.

Middle left Long section. White-collar functions are located in the prow of the building, the printing plant in the rear.

Bottom left Entrance-level plan. Editorial and advertising offices are arranged around a three-storey atrium.

Below Detailed wall section through the external wall showing the relationship between the tusk and glazing system.

Opposite below The building in 'full sail' dramatically exploits its hillside site. As at the Financial Times Print Works, the transparent exterior reveals the activities within.

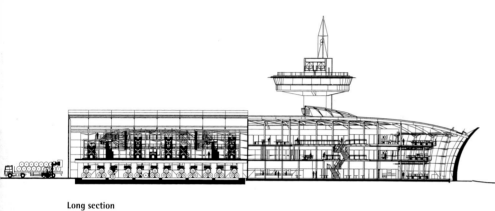

Long section

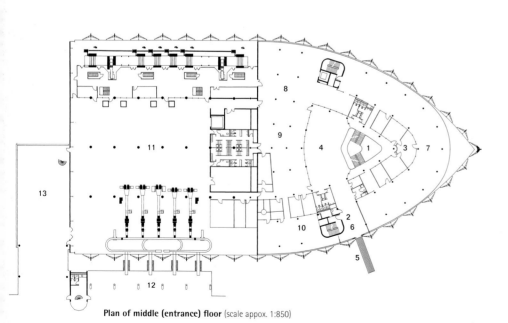

Plan of middle (entrance) floor (scale appox. 1:850)

Detailed section of wall and floor edges

Far right The apparently whimsical shape is highly functional; the outward curve of the walls is designed to reduce light reflection and glare.

Below Plan detail of tusk and bracket. The glass panels are supported using Planar bolts on a four-node connector. The cast-steel brackets resist horizontal wind loads.

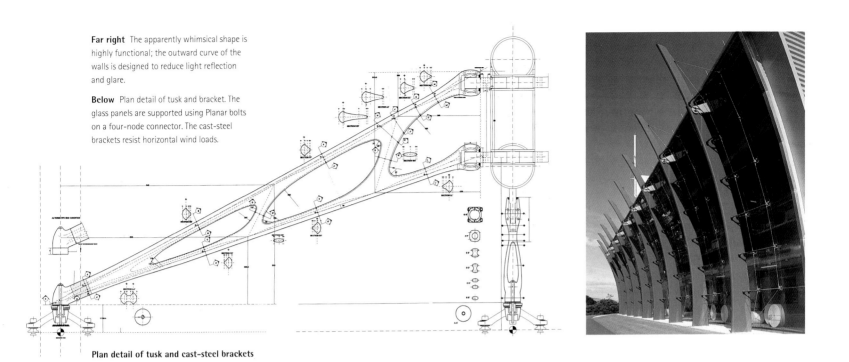

Plan detail of tusk and cast-steel brackets

National Gymnastics Centre

- Enric Miralles
- Alicante, Spain
- 1993

Top Detail of one of the cantilevered external canopies. Miralles' layering and fragmenting of elements gives the building an expressive complexity.

Above The cavernous interior of the main performance hall. The central structural spine is accentuated by canvas sheets hung on the underside of the roof. Reminiscent of circus tents and fairgrounds, the brightly coloured sheets add a festive air to the imposing spaces.

Opposite below West elevation. The tiered volume of the performance hall is clearly legible and the underside of the seating becomes a massive angled wall. The concrete A-frame supports the arrangement of steel trusses that make up the structural spine.

Barcelona-based architect Enric Miralles's vigorously convulsed organic buildings represent a very different sensibility from the city's contemporary school of sharply focused minimalism. His 'modern maximalism' embodies architecture at the limits of expression. Superficially, it appears to have an affinity with the arbitrary fragmentation of Deconstructivism, but its denser, richer, more fluid form-making has been seen by some critics as an extreme extension of the organic Modernism of Scharoun, Häring and Aalto.

With its tumbling, skewed forms and balletically contorted structure, the National Gymnastics Centre is the architectural manifestation of the activities it houses. Located in the southern coastal city of Alicante, the complex combines extensive practice and performance facilities for Spain's gymnasts, and was completed in time to host the 1993 International Championships. The commission was awarded to Miralles and his then partner Carme Pinós; together they had designed the archery range for the 1992 Barcelona Olympics, a dynamic reinterpretation of the conventional sports-building programme as a series of twisting, folding and interpenetrating bunkers. The gymnastics centre in Alicante is Miralles's largest project to date, and his expressive virtuosity here is no less apparent.

The site lies on the north side of a low hill, facing away from the sea and inland to the distant mountains of the Spanish tableland. The programme called for two large spaces – a hall for public performances that could hold four thousand people and a training hall. These are roughly organized in a T-shape with the competition hall forming the head and the training area the stem. With a maze of stairs, ramps and balconies overlooking both halls, the residual space between the two main volumes functions as a secondary circulation axis, extending in one direction to form a large canopy over the public entrance and in the other as a low roof of cascading folded planes over a smaller, secondary training hall. Spectators are generally confined to the upper levels, with the ground floor reserved for gymnasts. Public entry is by way of an enclosed drawbridge on the northwest side that climbs up from the street to meet a curved ramp that distributes spectators to their seats.

The sprawling assembly of angled walls, ramps, cantilevered canopies and inclined masts, combined with the textural variation of brick, raw concrete, glazing and coloured panels gives the complex a fractured, Cubist dynamism. The composition's unifying element is a low-pitched roof that enfolds the entire building in one continuous swoop. Expressed internally as an orientation device and externally as a dramatically undulating spine, the roof consists of three massive steel trusses running along the longitudinal axis, their jagged contours reflecting the mountains beyond. Dedicated to place and occasion, applying technology but not enslaved by it, the building embodies a radical yet lyrical vision.

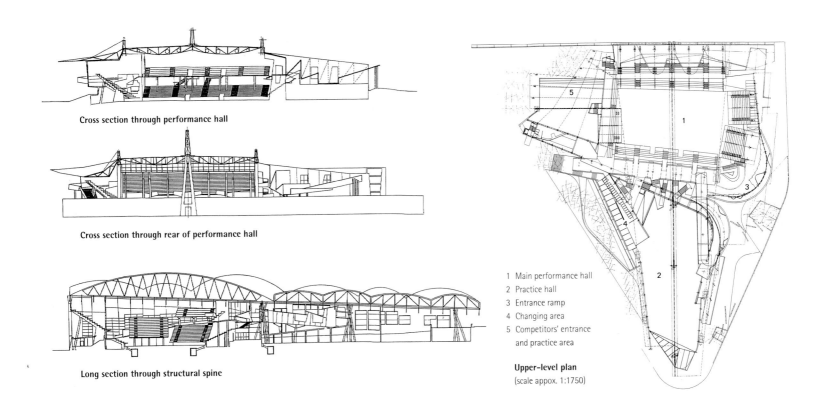

Cross section through performance hall

Cross section through rear of performance hall

Long section through structural spine

1 Main performance hall
2 Practice hall
3 Entrance ramp
4 Changing area
5 Competitors' entrance
   and practice area

Upper-level plan
(scale appox. 1:1750)

Left Looking north-west along the structural spine. The jagged, almost organic contours of the structure evocatively mirror the topography of the surrounding landscape.

Below Miralles's eloquent generative sketch of the building.

Bottom Site plan. The gymnastics centre joins a number of other sports facilities on the north side of a low hill on the edge of Alicante.

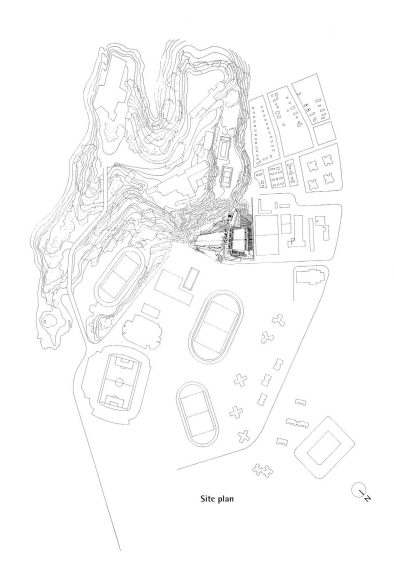

Site plan

Igus Factory

- Nicholas Grimshaw and Partners
- Cologne, Germany
- 1992

Above The roof is supported by vivid yellow pylons 31.5 metres high. The distinctive gravity-defying form of the steel pylons is reminiscent of the famous Skylon, originally designed for the Festival of Britain in 1951.

Opposite The eyeball-shaped roof domes provide smoke extraction as well as north light; in the event of a fire, the domes will soften and collapse, allowing heat to escape.

Below Perspective showing the modular, accretional character of the structure.

Founded in 1964 by production engineer Günter Blase, Igus is a family-run business specializing in supplying machine parts. Manufactured using innovative injection-moulding techniques, Igus products challenge conventional applications of plastics. Having outgrown its original headquarters, the company needed a flexible new building that could accommodate design development, offices, factory production and storage facilities, as well as being adaptable to future construction in phases as funds allowed. Impressed by Grimshaw's crisply detailed design for the Herman Miller Distribution Centre (completed in 1982), Blase turned up at Grimshaw's London office without an appointment and promptly offered him the commission.

The Igus building develops and refines themes of modularity and flexibility that have fascinated Grimshaw from his earliest days in practice. Environmental and production services are hung from the roof, allowing the floor area to be uninterrupted, a key stipulation of the brief. Administration facilities are housed in self-contained office pods on steel legs, which can be slotted in to the perimeter of the building or grouped together as required. The sleek metal cladding is also highly flexible, designed so that standard panels, windows and doors, may be easily interchanged. The structural system is based on a simple 11.25-metre-square grid, crowned with a distinctive eyeball-shaped roof dome that diffuses north light to all areas of the factory.

The building is envisaged as a series of phased accretions; when eventually completed, the Igus complex will comprise more than 24,000 square metres. The first 8,000-square-metre phase of the building is arranged in four sections, each with its own 18-metre-square landscaped courtyard in the centre. With their seasonally themed gardens the courtyards act as recreation and exhibition spaces. Dramatically poised pylons in the centre of each courtyard support the roof by means of four sets of tension rods positioned diagonally on plan. Painted a vivid cadmium yellow, the pylons have become an arresting corporate symbol, visible from both the adjacent motorway and the Cologne airport flight path.

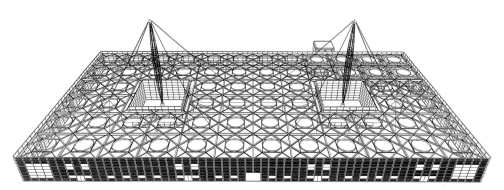

Perspective showing modular construction system

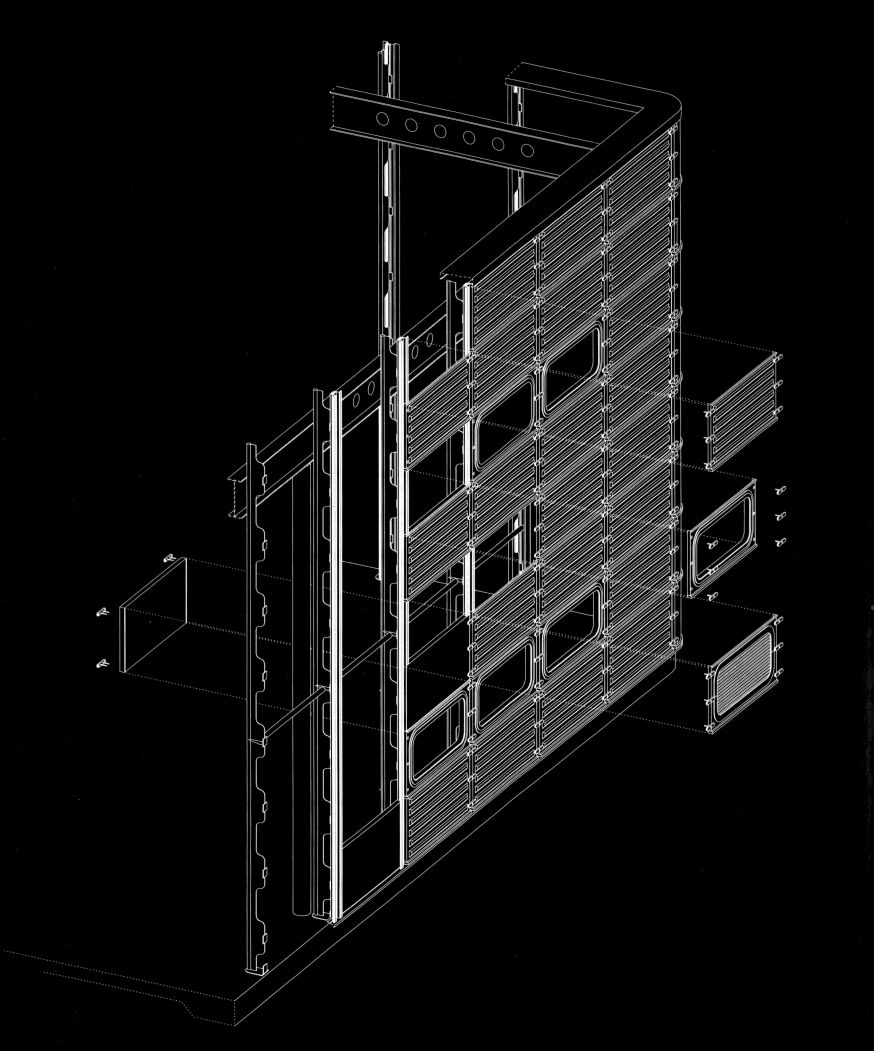

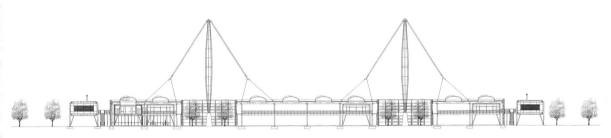

Cross section

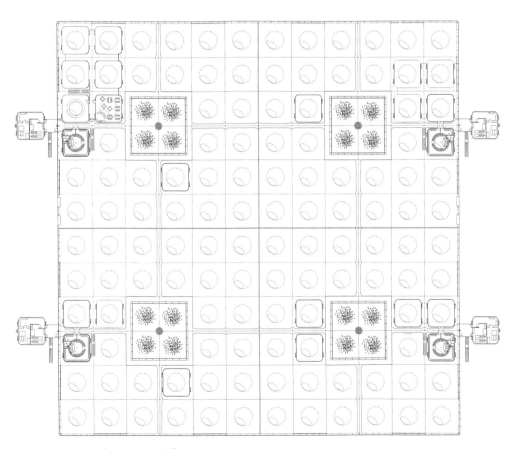

Floor plan (scale approx 1:1000)

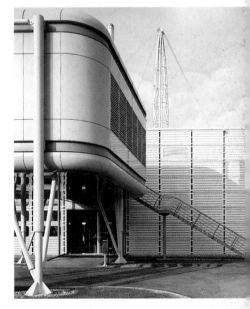

Alamillo Bridge

- Santiago Calatrava
- Seville, Spain
- 1992

Above The top of the massive pylon juts into the Sevillian sky like a periscope.

Below Site plan. The bridge forms part of a series of infrastructural improvements undertaken for Expo '92.

The staging of Expo '92 in Seville gave rise to ambitious improvements to the city's infrastructure, including regional road connections and a series of new bridges over the river Guadalquivir. One new road passes out of Seville to the north, across the Meandro San Jerónimo to the Isla de La Cartuja, skirting the Expo site and from there over the river Guadalquivir to the town of Camas. The unusual situation of crossing the river twice demanded a radical intervention.

Santiago Calatrava proposed two symmetrical bridges, each shaped like a giant harp. Although 1.5 kilometres apart, they would be angled towards each other to create what would appear from afar to be a monumental gateway in the Sevillian plain. Ultimately, only the bridge spanning the Meandro San Jerónimo was built.

Supported by a gargantuan inclined pylon, the asymmetrical, cable-stayed structure is an unmistakable landmark on the Expo site's north edge. The heroic tilt of the 142-metre-high pylon, poised like a rocket petrified at the moment of take-off, recalls the gravity-defying excesses of the famous Soviet Monument to Space Travel, in Moscow. The bridge deck spans 200 metres across the river and is supported by thirteen pairs of cable stays, tautly strung from the pylon. Dramatically angled at 58 degrees, the pylon is filled with concrete and clad in steel, its huge weight acting as a counterbalance.

The bridge deck is divided into three horizontal lanes and two vertical levels, with a pedestrian route above the traffic and sandwiched between the two lines of cables, which sets up tantalizing vistas for those crossing on foot. Unlike more conventional bridges, which tend to be monumental representations of structural behaviour, Calatrava's striking structures use the principles of engineering mechanics as a fertile basis for sculptural expression.

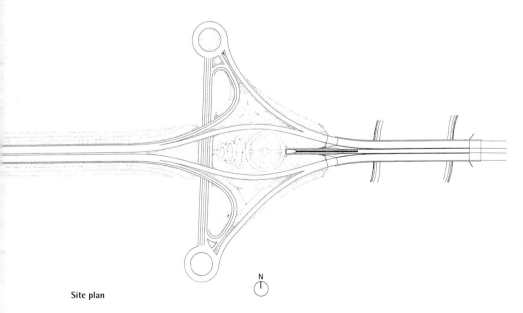

Site plan

N

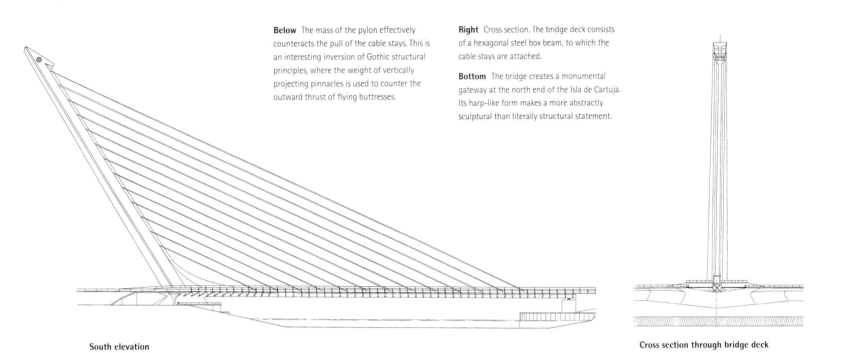

Below The mass of the pylon effectively counteracts the pull of the cable stays. This is an interesting inversion of Gothic structural principles, where the weight of vertically projecting pinnacles is used to counter the outward thrust of flying buttresses.

Right Cross section. The bridge deck consists of a hexagonal steel box beam, to which the cable stays are attached.

Bottom The bridge creates a monumental gateway at the north end of the Isla de Cartuja. Its harp-like form makes a more abstractly sculptural than literally structural statement.

South elevation

Cross section through bridge deck

Trinity Bridge

- Santiago Calatrava
- Salford, England
- 1995

Trinity Bridge spans the River Irwell, linking the Chapel Wharf area of Salford with the edge of Manchester's business district. Modest in scale, it is Santiago Calatrava's first completed project in Great Britain and represents a move away from the bent tube structures and concrete-support design that have preoccupied him in recent years. Drawing inspiration from the linear-sculptural constructions of Nuam Gabo and the spatial experiments of Antoine Pevsner, Calatrava's bridge is a confident exploration of lightweight materials and the aesthetics of visual tension, as well as a symbolic landmark in an underused area.

Rising from an in-situ concrete base, a sculptural 37-metre-high pylon supports both the subtly curved spanning bridge deck and the spiralling entry ramps by means of taut stainless-steel cable stays that gives the bridge its graceful, dynamic profile. The deck, made from an independent, torsionally stiffened hollow box girder beam, was lifted on site from the Salford side in three sections. Both the deck and the pylon were prefabricated in Bilbao, Spain, and assembled on site.

For Calatrava bridges are not merely utilitarian objects on the landscape, they have a social dimension, the power to bring communities together and heal past disputes. With the memorable Felipe II–Bach de Roda Bridge in Barcelona (1987), two distinct areas of the city were joined together, literally bridging the physical and social divides between the local populace. Likewise, Trinity Bridge is intended as a reconciling link between the cities of Salford and Manchester. At night its symbolic mission is emphasized when both the white pylon and the underside of the bridge are illuminated, reflecting a dramatic play of light on to the river surface.

Site plan

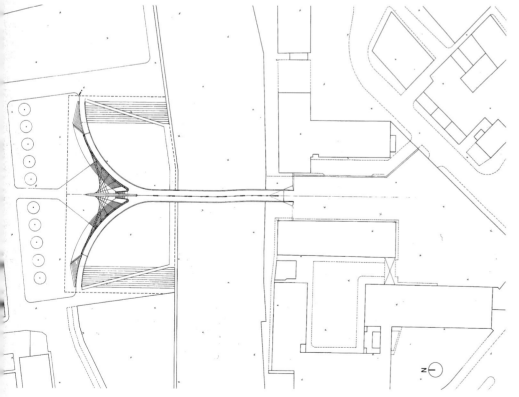

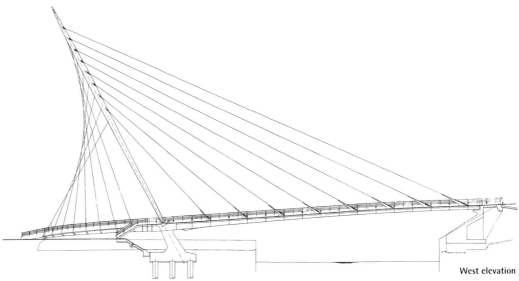

West elevation

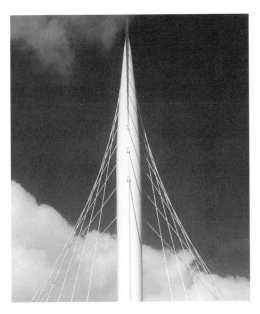

Opposite above Detail of the steel pylon and the delicate network of cable stays.

Opposite below Site plan. The 67-metre-wide bridge spans the River Irwell, connecting a new car parking area to the edge of Manchester's thriving business district.

Top West elevation. The difference in height between the two banks of the river is ingeniously overcome by Calatrava's design: the bridge deck has a gentle pitch of 1:18.

Above The tensile lightness and grace of the cable stays elevates the bridge from the status of mere utility to the realm of visual poetry.

Right Two curving ramps lead to the bridge deck. The stainless-steel cable stays were positioned and post-tensioned after final computer verification of lengths.

Exhibition Hall

- Thomas Herzog
- Linz, Austria
- 1994

Above Detail of the steel arch structure. Each arch is made up of four 900 x 600 mm box sections, which were welded together on site and finished with an epoxy paint treatment.

Opposite, above left The ground-floor plan illustrates the arrangement of the three main exhibition halls.

Opposite, above right Cut-away isometric of part of the barrel vault structure. The steel arches are paired at expansion joints.

Opposite, below The seemingly infinite and surprisingly translucent volume of the exhibition hall. Natural light is filtered through specially developed glazed roof panels containing grids that diffuse natural light.

Below The rhythm of the partially exposed steel arches articulates the monolithic volume of the barrel vault. Situated amid nondescript surroundings, the exhibition hall makes a powerful impact.

Situated on the banks of the Danube, Linz once boasted a thriving iron and steel industry, but today it is in decline, and the city is suffering the social and environmental consequences. In an attempt to revive investment and employment opportunities, an architectural competition was held in the late 1980s for a hotel and multipurpose exhibition centre. Drawing on the region's expertise in steel manufacturing, the brief stipulated that the building's structure should play a prominent part in any solution. The commission was won by Thomas Herzog, working in collaboration with engineers Sailer & Stepan.

Linz Design Centre occupies a nondescript site south of the city centre. Consisting of an eight-storey hotel and vast exhibition and conference centre arranged around a paved square, the complex might be overlooked as another middle-European business park, were it not for the striking volume of the exhibition hall. An immense,

gestural building, it demonstrates Herzog's rigorous concern for materials and how they are put together.

The underlying element of the programme was flexibility. The 208-metre-long building is essentially a series of adaptable spaces – ranging from a 650-seat congress room and a 1200-seat events hall to a conference room for up to 800 and associated cellular ancillary spaces – that can be interconnected as required. This vast agglomeration is elegantly enveloped by a shallow barrel-vaulted structure that was able to absorb five internal layout changes during the design phase. A total of thirty-four swooping steel ribs, 13 metres high, span an area the size of two football fields. Czech steel was used to fabricate the arches, although an Austrian company organized the site work.

The combination of the vault's sleek transparency and Herzog's precise detailing instils a functional, monolithic form with drama and refinement. Natural light is exploited as much as possible to avoid reducing the interiors to featureless, disorienting caverns. Like a huge greenhouse, the building is covered in glazed panels that were specially developed for the project. A sandwich of two insulating glass sheets encloses a 16-millimetre-thick retro-reflecting grid, enabling indirect light to pass through the panel. Direct light is blocked, however, so the effects of overheating and glare are minimized. Computers calculated the position of the grid relative to the angle of the sun, so that no two panels are the same.

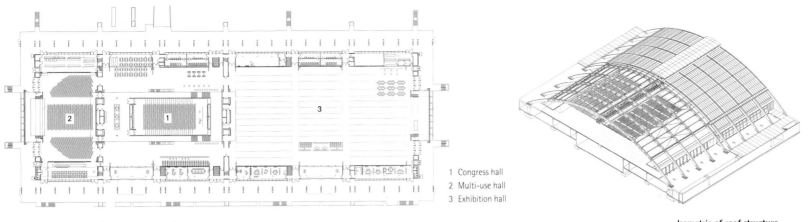

Ground-floor plan (scale approx. 1:1850)

1 Congress hall
2 Multi-use hall
3 Exhibition hall

Isometric of roof structure

RAC Regional Control Centre

- Nicholas Grimshaw and Partners
- Bristol, England
- 1995

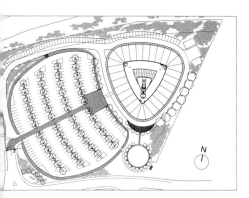

Site plan

Top The Control Centre is topped by a steel spire, which acts as a highly visible corporate landmark. Suspended from the spire is the customer visiting room.

Above Site plan. The building is set in a landscaped bowl that helps to improve the microclimate around it and insulates the ground level from the noise of the adjacent motorway. Enclosed by protecting hornbeam hedges, the car park is laid out axially on the entrance to the building.

Just before the M4 motorway crosses the River Severn into Wales it intersects with the M5 on the edge of Bristol in a tangled intestine of tarmac and interminable stream of cars. Presiding over these throbbing slipways is the RAC Regional Control Centre, the first of the British motoring organization's high-profile nerve centres, which will be stationed at similarly strategic intersections across the country. Designed by Nicholas Grimshaw and Partners, the building's antecedents are immediately recognizable in the Western Morning News headquarters (page 22) outside Plymouth. Whereas Western Morning News is clearly a liner in dry dock, however, the RAC building is more like a spacecraft, its otherworldly formal and technical sophistication transcending its humdrum surroundings.

The building adopts a simple equilateral triangle plan, with gently curving sides suggesting movement, streamlining and, tangentially, flying saucers. The shimmering faceted glass walls are articulated by *brises soleil* that line each floor level. Strung from a cat's cradle of tensile wires, the lightweight mesh louvres are designed to combat glare on computer screens inside. Less three-dimensionally gymnastic than Western Morning News, the RAC building has a less frenetic function; this is an exclusively corporate domain, no conflation of blue-and-white-collar operations here.

Three floors of offices are wrapped around a central void containing an impressively choreographed staircase. Overlooked by an inner ring of cellular meeting rooms, the atrium also functions as the building's social centre. The corporate focal point is provided by a 65-metre-high steel mast that rises from the centre of the plan to support an elevated chamber (in the manner of the Western Morning News boardroom/bridge). This is the customer visiting room, which is linked by an umbilical lift and staircase to the rest of the building and affords panaromic views of the surrounding trafficscape.

Visible for miles around, the two pronged steel mast towers project above the suspended eyrie like a tuning fork. At night the building's confident, glowing presence (it is a 24-hour hive of activity) cannot fail to reassure and inspire even the most weary motorist.

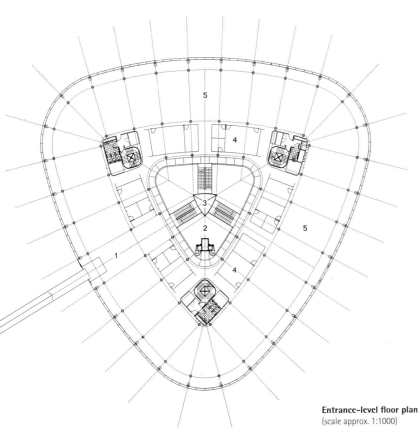

1 Entrance foyer
2 Atrium
3 Staircase
4 Cellular offices
5 Open-plan offices

Entrance-level floor plan
(scale approx. 1:1000)

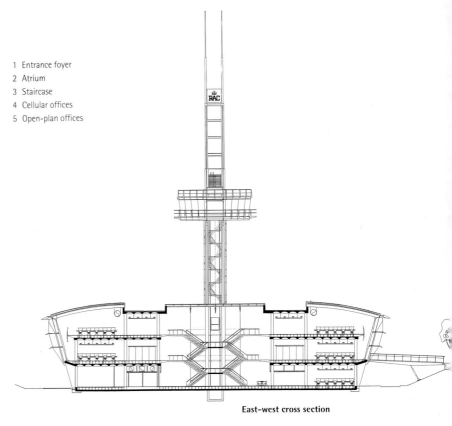

East-west cross section

Top left The concentric triangular plan facilitates circulation routes and the inter-relation of departments. 7000 square metres of office accommodation is arranged over three floors that wrap around a central atrium,

Top right East-west cross section through the offices and atrium. The entrance bridge docks into the building on the first floor.

Left The outward-tilting external walls are shaded with external walkways designed to provide both maintenance access and act as sun louvres.

Above left With its network of interconnecting stairs, the atrium is the social and functional hub of the building,

Above right Detail of the elevated entrance bridge and the specially developed glazing for the upper two floors. The double-glazed, trapezoidal units are angled and faceted to accommodate the profile of the building.

Wilkahn Factory

- Thomas Herzog
- Bad Munder, Germany
- 1993

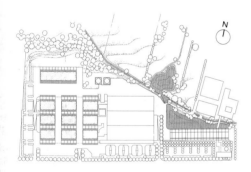

Site plan

Top Detail of one of the four structural naves. Laminated timber, tensile steel rods, glazed and translucent panels combine to create a crisply integrated whole.

Above Site plan of the Wilkahn campus. Herzog's building adjoins an existing production hall and forms the prototype in a proposed sequence of similar units. (Three future extensions are shown in a light tint.)

Opposite Part of the south elevation with its photovoltaic canopy and the long west elevation with its translucent insulation panels. As well as being a boldly industrial expression of structure and materials, the building embodies new ideas about the relationship of the manufacturing process to the natural environment.

The German contract furniture manufacturer Wilkahn has its headquarters in rolling green fields southwest of Hanover in northern Germany. Since the firm was founded in 1907 it has steadily expanded its operations, resulting in a collection of historically diverse and disparately situated buildings. Thomas Herzog was commissioned to rationalize the entire plant and to design successive building phases for future expansion.

His first addition is a striking production hall, located on the western boundary of the site, which houses facilities for table-top production, chair assembly and upholstery-making. These functions relate to work carried out in other parts of the complex, so the new factory is linked to neighbouring production halls. Initial sketches show the genesis of the structural concept – three roof girders carried between four humanoid 'carpenters' – which has been evocatively realized in the finished building. The carpenters are transformed into four naves, with laminated timber beams hung between them. Slender steel chords are attached to the bottom of each beam to improve their structural effectiveness, a principle clearly expressed on the elevations. The steel tension elements are painted a vivid blue to emphasize the dynamic structure. From a distance the quartet of soaring naves seem to break up the scale of the huge production hall so that it becomes comparable in massing to the brick terraces of the surrounding village. The naves also give the building a muscular, industrial rhythm.

The naves divide the airy, daylight-filled interior into three distinct production areas; each area in turn contains administration and rest facilities. A reflection of Wilkahn's non-hierarchical management philosophy, this democratic configuration heightens the sense of territorial and team identity for groups of workers. Continuous eye-level strips of glass afford views over the surrounding countryside; the windows can also be opened to provide manual cross ventilation.

The building's long east and west façades are clad in rectangular double-glazed panels, between which translucent insulation material is sandwiched to protect against heat gain during the summer. The insulation also disperses glare, while admitting a soft, diffuse light in the manner of Japanese *shoji* (rice-paper) screens. Seen from the outside at night, the hall's luminous walls glow with a surprising radiance. The two short side elevations are infilled with a combination of glazing and insulation sandwich panels faced in larch boarding.

Herzog's building is a thoughtful resolution of functional, aesthetic and ecological concerns. His continual experimentation with energy-saving devices manifests itself here in the photovoltaic cells containing sheets of amorphous silicone that are integrated into the south elevation's glass canopy. Though only at the prototype stage, the cells generate sufficient energy to power the factory's forklift trucks.

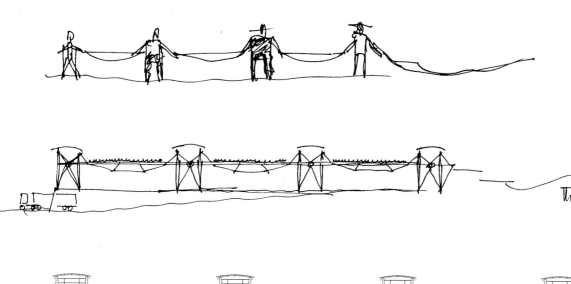

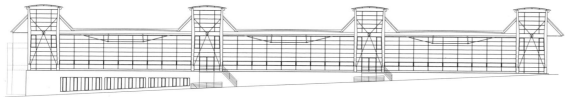

Left, top to bottom Herzog's initial sketch of a quartet of humanoid 'carpenters' holding up a building bears a satisfying resemblance to the final structural form. The carpenters evolved into naves that not only act as structural elements but also demarcate the internal production hall space into identifiable sections.

Below The south-west corner. To accommodate the slightly sloping site the building sits on a concrete plinth that varies in height along its length.

West elevation

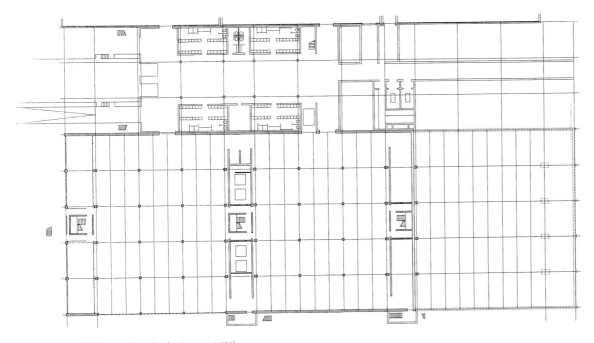

Left Plinth-level plan showing the new production hall connecting with an existing building.

Left, middle and bottom Dissected isometric projections of the laminated timber naves and intermediate steel structure. Their interaction creates a functional yet elegantly rhythmical composition .

Below Detailed section through the west wall consisting of a timber frame infilled with translucent insulating sandwich panels. The panels diffuse glare and prevent heat build-up in warm weather. Manually openable windows at eye level provide natural cross ventilation.

Plinth-level floor plan (scale appox. 1:600)

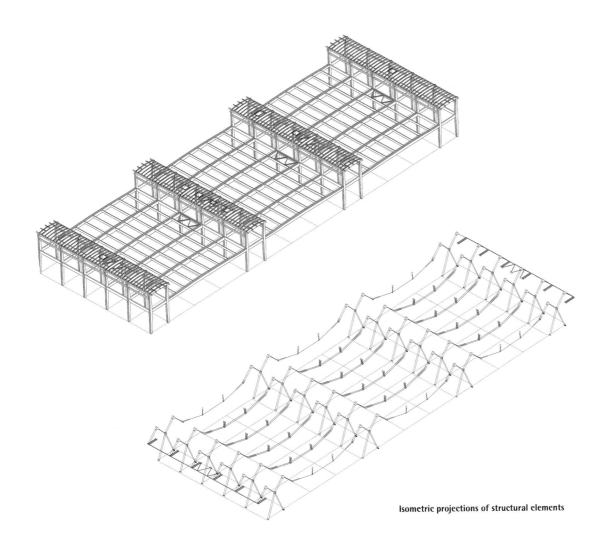

Isometric projections of structural elements

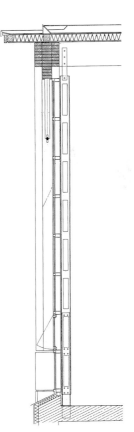

Detailed section of west wall

Museum of Fruit

- Itsuko Hasegawa
- Yamanashi, Japan
- 1996

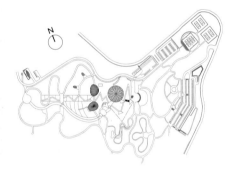

Site plan

Top The delicate deformed lattice structure of the greenhouse that forms part of the overall Fruit Museum complex is a contemporary reinterpretation of the traditional glass house typology.

Above Site plan. The trio of globular forms – greenhouse, event space and workshop – are scattered around the site in an apparently random, natural fashion.

Opposite The spectacular terrace restaurant at the top of the workshop building. As plants are trained up the enclosing lattice, it will eventually act as a pergola.

Lying to the west of Tokyo, Yamanashi Prefecture is one of the most intensive fruit-producing areas in Japan. Inspired by the region's geography and economy, the local authorities commissioned Itsuko Hasegawa to design a group of buildings dedicated to the study of fruit and fruit culture. The Museum of Fruit is a trio of hemispherical forms scattered apparently at random around the site like partially buried fruit seeds. Two of the lightweight steel structures are glazed – one houses a tropical greenhouse, the other is an event space – while the third consists of a basketlike frame around a four-storey workshop.

Containing a lush array of tropical fruit trees and plants, the main building is a deformed globe 20 metres high. The structure's shape represents a fruit seed's mature image and the beginning of a new cycle of life. A saucer-shaped dome contains the event space, supported by steel members that radiate fluidly from a central core. Within this low-slung structure is a raised stage for lectures and performances, surrounded by planting. The luminous event space and the globular greenhouse are linked by a subterranean exhibition hall.

The complex's third component, a multistorey workshop, is a transparent rectilinear building encased in a lopsided, egg-shaped steel lattice, which acts as a pergola that will eventually be colonized by fruit-bearing lianas. Workshops and offices occupy the lower levels, with a roof terrace and restaurant above. The building

contrasts with the other two structures functionally and morphologically, symbolizing the 'foreignness' inherent in the vitality and continuity of nature. Externally, the buildings are linked by paths sheltered by jaunty arcades of perforated mesh, a favourite Hasegawa material. At night, the three deformed hemispheres glow with a strange and beautiful intensity and reveal the intricacy of their structures.

The buildings' organic geometry was developed using sophisticated computer modelling by a team of structural and seismic engineers from Ove Arup & Partners. To create the desired degree of asymmetry, simple hemispherical shapes were progressively distorted into complex volumes. Once the desired forms were reached, their structural behaviour was investigated for strength, eccentricity, stability against snap-through buckling (when a shell curves inward like a partly inflated football) and for controlling movement to limit glass breakage in an earthquake. Despite the complexities of the design process, the structures are remarkably simple.

Hasegawa's approach to architecture is an expressive synthesis of technology and nature. From a distance the museum resembles three drops of water resting lightly on the sloping hillside. Yet because the shapes of the three buildings are not perfectly Euclidean, their sensuous deformities reflect the influence of gravity and wind. Instead of seeing technology and nature as antagonists, Hasegawa regards them as reciprocal forces.

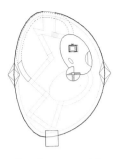

Greenhouse ground-floor plan
(scale appox. 1:1000)

Below Luxuriant plantings fill the greenhouse. The meticulously engineered structure, which is inspired by organic forms, epitomizes Hasegawa's highly expressive synthesis of nature and technology.

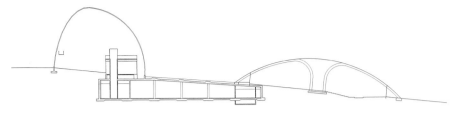

Cross section through greenhouse and event space

Above, left to right Plans and section of the greenhouse and event space show them linked at basement level by a subterranean exhibition hall.

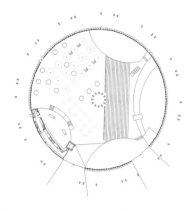

Event space ground-floor plan (scale appox. 1:1000)

Above The tree-like structure of the event space features a series of swooping steel arches radiating out from the central core. Timber was originally considered as a possible material but did not have the required structural capacity. Japanese building codes, which include such factors as seismic loading, are very exacting.

Workshop first-floor plan
(scale appox. 1:1000)

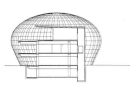

Cross section through workshop

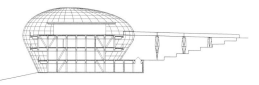

Long section through workshop

Above The workshop building enclosed by its steel lattice structure, with the greenhouse to the left. A kinked bridge supported on robotic legs leads to the upper part of the hillside site.

Left Plan and sections through the workshop building show how it relates to the site.

Following page Glowing in the dusk, the trio of buildings reveals the ingenious and poetic complexity of their respective structures.

Sculpting with Light

The glazed façade of the Law Faculty building
at Cambridge, by Foster and Partners
(page 54)

Law Faculty

- Foster and Partners
- Cambridge, England
- 1995

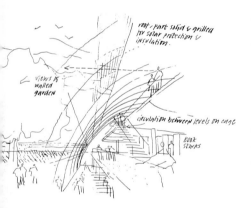

Top The tapering corner of the Law Faculty building, with its entrance marked by a spindly steel column. Stirling's iconic History Faculty is just across the precinct on the left.

Above Foster's generative sketch crystallizes the notion of the transparent vault overlooking the garden.

Opposite The luminous, wedge-shaped atrium that acts as entrance, meeting place and collecting point for the entire building.

Tactfully inserted into the town's evolving Sidgwick Avenue campus just west of the River Cam, the Law Faculty building is, surprisingly, the first Cambridge excursion for Foster and Partners. Although the university's ancient fabric is studded with modern interventions, some are more successful than others. As a confident, expressive articulation of space and structure, however, the Law Faculty must rank as one of the more distinguished additions to Cambridge's uneven contemporary canon.

Responding to the particularities of its surroundings, the Law Faculty reinstates a coherent north-south axis through the site. Its splayed west side creates a breathing space – not quite courtyard, not quite square – in which the campus's disparate elements can coexist. The angular corner marks the entrance, which is further emphasized by the totemic presence of a slender steel column.

Containing a mixture of lecture halls, seminar rooms and library facilities, the building is a cool antidote to its most directly confrontational neighbour, James Stirling's glowering red brick History Faculty (1967) on the adjoining west site. Through a crisply minimalist elevation of reconstituted stone and Cambridge-blue opaque-glass panels on the south elevation, Foster's building also succeeds in establishing a dialogue with Casson Conder's raised faculty block.

So far, the Law Faculty might be regarded simply as an elegant contextual exercise. On the north side, however, a steel-and-glass vault – neither window nor wall nor roof, but a skilfully engineered hybrid of all three – billows out over a mature garden. Like a giant conservatory, the curved glass skin encloses and exposes the four library floors and student activity. Inside, regimented rows of reader tables – based on the desks in the Foster office – and solid birch bookstacks are drenched in north light. Devised in collaboration with YRM Anthony Hunt Associates, the vault is supported by a triangulated-steel Vierendeel structure, cylindrical in section, to which the glazed panels are fixed. The triangular format also allows the repetitive use of a single panel, thus maximizing component efficiency.

The library floors are cantilevered off five raking concrete columns that rise at an angle through the building. Remarkably, the concrete was cast in situ; the pristinely smooth finish was achieved by steel shuttering and the addition of Scottish granite aggregate. Cast within the columns are conduits for communications, fire alarm and security systems.

In a formal set piece reminiscent of the Carré d'art at Nîmes (page 116), the main staircase tumbles theatrically through a void down to the entrance foyer; below ground are a cafe and trio of lecture theatres. The entrance atrium forms an appropriate prelude to the drama within: Foster's unerring sense of spatial dynamism combined with tectonic ingenuity has produced a notable Cambridge first.

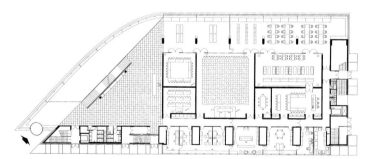

Ground-floor plan (scale approx. 1:750)

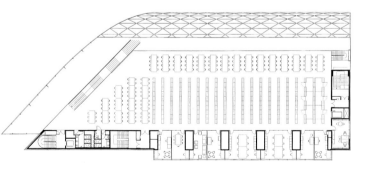

Typical library-level plan

Opposite, above The imposing library vault consists of a steel Vierendeel structure infilled with identical triangular glazed panels for maximum structural efficiency. The system was specially devised in collaboration with YRM Anthony Hunt Associates.

Opposite, below As the building tapers to a point, a wedge-shaped atrium is created.

Left The prow-like entrance is animated by student activity.

Below left Site plan of the Sidgwick Avenue campus. The Law Faculty responds sensitively to its context, reinstating a coherent north-south axis through the site. To the south is Casson Conder's raised faculty block.

Below right The more introverted south elevation is clad in reconstituted Portland stone and opaque glass panels.

Bottom The cross section shows the cantilevered library floors and lecture theatre (one of three) at basement level.

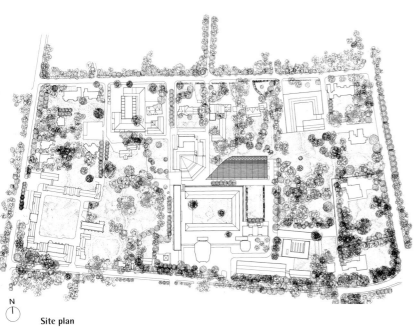

Site plan

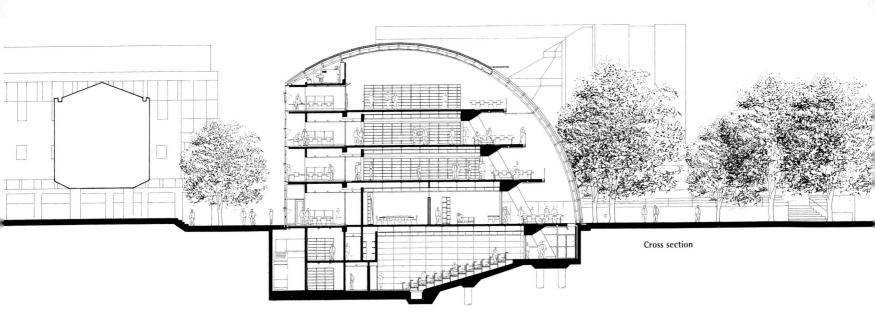

Cross section

Secondary School

- Helmut Richter
- Vienna, Austria
- 1995

Top Part of the crystalline flank of the south elevation, which gives the building a startling, amorphous quality.

Above The school in its suburban context. The two sloping glass roofs enclose an entrance hall and sports hall.

Opposite Part of the external recreation area between the two halls. A new type of glazing developed by the Austrian firm of Brüder Eckelt was used to achieve the required degree of seamlessness and transparency. It resembles the Planar system, except that the stainless-steel brackets are fixed only to the inner sheet (of laminated safety glass). The outer sheet (of toughened safety glass) is connected to the inner one at its edges. The outcome is a glacially smooth external skin.

For the first time since the 1920s Vienna is expanding. As a result of political changes in eastern Europe, the Austrian capital now finds that it needs to service the requirements of a growing population. Around forty new schools are planned to improve the city's educational facilities, and enlightened municipal patronage has commissioned a range of notable Austrian architects to design the new buildings. They include Helmut Richter, who has completed an extraordinary school in Waldhausenstrasse in Vienna's 14th district.

Although based in Vienna, Richter neither grapples with the city's monumental history as Deconstructivists Coop Himmelb(l)au do, nor does he engage in Hans Hollein–style games of complex ambiguity. To some extent Richter builds in Vienna as if Vienna did not exist. His architecture is a distillation of rigorously applied technology closely allied with the engineering sensibility of many contemporary British and French architects.

The Waldhausenstrasse school is Richter's largest and possibly most spectacular project to date. The site lies on a steep south-facing slope. The plan is essentially straightforward, a logical comb arrangement that evolves out of the building's functions. Three ribs of teaching and communal accommodation run up the slope; the outer two contain classrooms, the middle one common areas, such as the library, refectory, laboratories and workshops.

The ribs are joined at their southern ends by a narrow spine of horizontal and vertical circulation. Docked on to the south side of the spine are two glazed volumes, like giant conservatories that house the entrance hall and the school's gymnasium.

The south elevation has a seamless, crystalline smoothness, like an intensely blue iceberg. The exterior's amorphousness has made the building a source of local controversy, but its wilful external form is balanced by the interior's transparency and spatial dynamism. A bridge leads to an understated entrance in the building's glassy flank, which opens into the large, luminous volume of the entrance hall. Supported on delicately tapering steel trusses, the glass roof slopes dramatically from a four-storey high apex. Tiers of walkways in the circulation spine lead across to the classroom wings and connect the entrance hall with the gymnasium, the building's exhilarating centrepiece. The span is longer than the entrance hall, but again the structure is surprisingly minimal: paired steel rafters are supported by inclined tubular-steel struts that spring up from the spine. A glazed screen follows the angle of the struts, creating a trapezoidal section for the sports hall and generating an interplay between the various departments of the school and the life of the city, which can be surveyed from the spine walkways.

Right The cross section reveals the relationship between the four-storey classroom block and the angular volume of the sports hall. The two elements are linked by a central circulation spine.

Below right Three finger-like blocks of classrooms and common facilities connect with one side of the circulation spine. On the other are the giant conservatories of the sports hall and entrance hall.

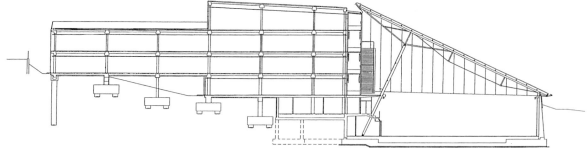

Cross section

1 Circulation spine
2 Common facilities
3 Classroom blocks
4 Sports hall roof
5 External recreation terrace
6 Entrance hall roof

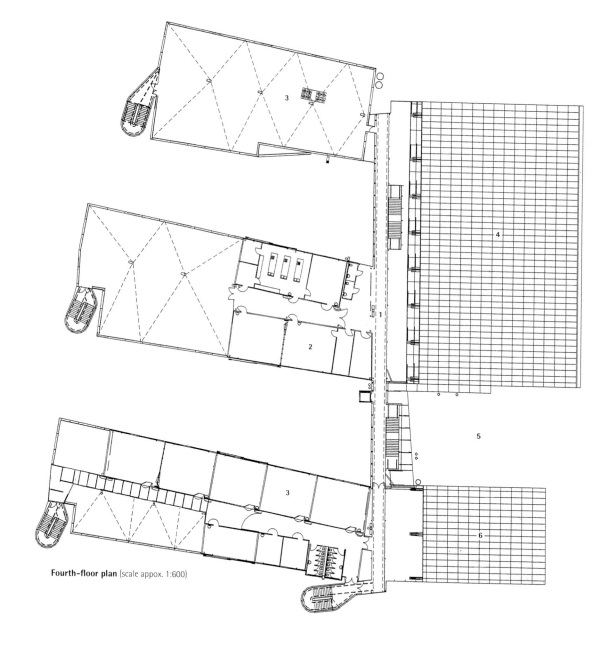

Fourth-floor plan (scale appox. 1:600)

Below Detail of the surprisingly slender roof structure of the sports hall. The size of structural members is reduced as far as possible to create an impression of lightness and dematerialization.

Below right Part of the spatially dramatic circulation spine with walkways overlooking the sports hall. The external recreation space and the glazed volume of the entrance hall are also visible.

Bottom right The light-filled sports hall. The hall faces south, so control of heat gain and ventilation are critical. The outer layer of glass has a solar control coating, giving some protection from insolation and glare, as well as generating the intense blue of the exterior. Hot air is expelled at the apexes of the sloping glass roofs by an automatically variable ventilation system; blinds can also be lowered to reduce glare and heat gain.

Museum of Glass

- Design Antenna
- Kingswinford, England
- 1995

Top Detail of the junction between the laminated glass beams and the glass columns. This prototypical project exploits the compressive potential of glass; it is a relatively simple step from the use of a glass fin as a stiffener and bracing device to its use as a column.

Above A poetic fusion of light and space, the jewel-like pavilion epitomizes the Modernist goal of transparency.

In both form and content the national Museum of Glass at Kingswinford in England's West Midlands is an eloquent expression of the human preoccupation with glass. Ever since the Egyptians first fused vitreous surfaces onto stone and clay in around 1500 BC, glass has assumed myriad decorative and functional forms, but here it makes a transcendental leap into the realm of structural material.

The museum's siting is apt, for the nearby town of Stourbridge has been associated with English glass-making for four hundred years, particularly during the nineteenth century, when an extraordinary spirit of invention and artistry prevailed. The collection of eighteenth- and nineteenth-century glass is set out in the refurbished galleries of Broadfield House, a handsome early nineteenth-century mansion with a Palladian façade. At the back of the house is a new public entrance, with various amenities, including a glass-blowing workshop, arranged around a courtyard.

The entrance is housed in a rectangular, flat-roofed pavilion constructed entirely from glass. Quietly exuding Miesian simplicity and poetic transparency, it belies the calculated ingenuity of its architect, Brent Richards, of Design Antenna, and engineer Tim Macfarlane, of Dewhurst Macfarlane. The glass-panelled skin is supported on a triple-laminated-glass structural frame. Laminated-glass beams at 1.1-metre centres span 5.7 metres from the rear brick wall to a series of glass columns on the front elevation. The delicate fin-shaped columns are set in metal shoes below ground and connected to the beams by means of bonded mortice-and-tenon joints.

Believed to be the largest all-glass building at the time of writing, the structure is remarkably robust: an earlier prototype for a small conservatory (designed by Rick Mather and engineered by Macfarlane using the same system) withstood the weight of a somewhat surprised fleeing burglar. A combination of fritted and low-emissivity glass contrives to drastically reduce the effects of solar gain. The pavilion has an exquisite miragelike seamlessness – it barely seems there, yet it marks an intriguing new phase in the evolution of glass.

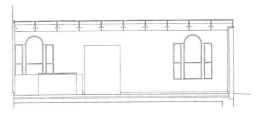

Long section

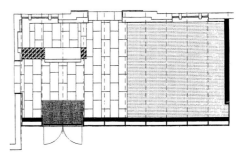

Ground-floor plan (scale approx. 1:200)

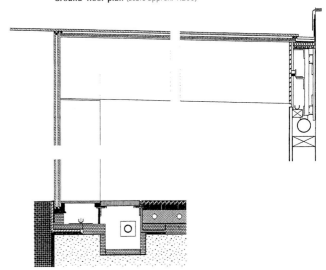

Detailed cross section

Top Long section and ground-floor plan showing how the pavilion docks on to the side of the existing museum.

Above Detailed cross section through the pavilion. The triple-laminated glass beams span from the existing rear back wall to glass columns set in metal shoes below ground. The beams and columns were custom-made. A heating unit is concealed under the limestone floor.

Left The transparent wall plane is made up of three layers of glass. An outer, low emissivity layer reduces solar gain and is separated from the two inner panes of toughened glass by a 10-mm air gap. The roof uses a similar construction, but the inner layer has a pattern of ceramic bars fritted on to it to diffuse heat gain and glare. In very hot weather an air-extract system can also be used.

Cy Twombly Gallery

- Renzo Piano Building Workshop
- Houston, United States
- 1995

Above The new galleries are a fitting setting for Cy Twombly's Abstract Expressionist works.

Below Detail of the multilayered roof structure, which incorporates an elaborate light and sun-shading system.

Opposite, above The site plan of the Menil campus shows the new building in relation to the existing Menil Collection. The floor plan, far right, shows the simple interlocking arrangement of galleries.

Opposite, below left The lightweight louvres contrast with the solidity of the walls.

Opposite, above right The finely honed pavilion in its campus-like setting.

Following on from the building he designed for the Menil Collection in 1987, Renzo Piano was commissioned by Dominque de Menil to design this smaller gallery dedicated to the paintings, drawings and sculptures of one of America's leading Abstract Expressionists. The Cy Twombly Gallery and the Menil Collection are separated by a street's width in Houston's residential Melrose district, but each has a distinct character: Piano's first building is essentially an elongated villa with lush loggias and courtyards, whereas the newer gallery is an austere, elemental structure, like a temple.

Although compact, the sharp refinement of the Twombly Gallery's precast concrete walls sets it apart from its neighbours. The plan is based on a simple grid of nine squares – the geometry was originally conceived by Twombly – with two bays joined together to accommodate larger canvases. In three dimensions, the two-dimensional grid becomes an interlocking set of elegantly proportioned cubes, with cool plaster walls and warm oak floors. Changes in the scale and orientation of the doorways between each gallery subtly suggest a sense of diversity within the uniform framework.

Like 'a butterfly alighting on a firm surface' – as Piano describes it – a floating, cantilevered roof conceived as a series of diaphanous layers rests delicately on the concrete block walls' solid mass. Daylight is filtered through an intricate system of roof grilles, louvres and tinted-glass panels developed in collaboration with Ove Arup & Partners, diffusing the intensity of Houston's southern light into an exquisitely luminous wash. The roof's bottom layer consists of a seamless white-cotton scrim stretched taut like a painter's canvas to form the ceiling. Woven in Belgium, the fabric was installed by local sailmakers using traditional marine technology of grommets and turnbuckles.

As visitors stroll through the sequence of galleries, they remain blissfully unaware of the complex layers of construction above their heads. In conception and execution the building has a finely honed, abstract quality worthy of Twombly's enigmatic paintings. As Dominique de Menil remarked approvingly, 'Piano has built a jewel'.

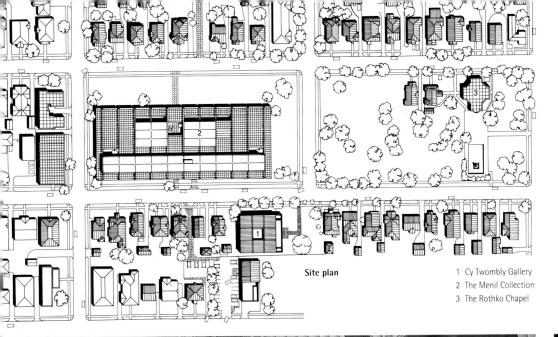

Site plan

1 Cy Twombly Gallery
2 The Menil Collection
3 The Rothko Chapel

Floor plan (scale approx. 1:300)

1 Galleries
2 Archive
3 Entrance Foyer
4 Alcove

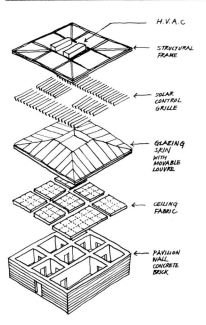

H.V.A.C

STRUCTURAL FRAME

SOLAR CONTROL GRILLE

GLAZING SKIN WITH MOVABLE LOUVRE

CEILING FABRIC

PAVILION WALL CONCRETE BRICK

Exploded conceptual sketch of gallery roof

Cy Twombly Gallery • 65

Cartier Foundation

- Jean Nouvel, Emmanuel Cattani and Associates
- Paris, France
- 1994

Top Banks of external wall-climber lifts glide up the rear elevation. Normally, centrally located lift cores provide structural bracing; here they are removed to the perimeter, and steel cross-bracing is instead provided at each end of the building.

Above Seen from the Boulevard Raspail the traditional urban character of Paris dissolves and the building appears as a series of transparent planes merging with the surrounding trees.

Located in Paris's 14th arrondissement, close to the Montparnasse cemetery, the Cartier Foundation does not immediately register as a building. Rather, constrasting with the city's solidly reassuring urban texture, it appears as a minimal glass block, or a series of exquisitely transparent planes set in a mature garden, a finely honed exercise in the poetry of abstraction. Nouvel's other famous Parisian set piece is the Institut du Monde Arabe, a tautly chiselled sliver of a building, equipped with a modern, environmentally responsive version of a traditional *mashrabiya* screen wall. In this project he reveals his experimentation with the notion of architecture dematerializing, 'blurring the tangible limits of the building', as he describes it. His Tour Sans Fin project was a proposal for a slender tower the height of the World Trade Centre, its transparent upper storeys dissolving into the sky.

The scale of the Cartier building, however, is decidedly more modest, yet the building's insubstantial appearance is deceptive. It combines seven floors of offices for the Cartier Foundation, the artistic trust endowed by the international jeweller and watchmaker, with public galleries of contemporary art on the ground and lower ground floors. Below these are another six levels of car parking, plant and storage spaces.

The site once contained the palace and garden of Napoleon's diplomat Chateaubriand, and all thirty-seven of the mature trees in the garden were protected by conservation orders. In addition, local planners insisted that any intervention must occupy the same narrow footprint as the previous building. The outcome is that eight of the Cartier Foundation's sixteen stories are sunk underground.

Nouvel has created a vast, luxurious shop front on the Boulevard Raspail that displays both the building and the garden to heightened advantage. A free-standing glass screen, eight metres high, replaces the site's original blind perimeter walls. One of Chateaubriand's mighty cedars guards the entrance, its brooding, organic presence set against Nouvel's diaphanous planes and volumes. The building is framed by two sheer glass walls that project three bays beyond its perimeter and one bay above its roof, dissolving its mass in a mesmeric play of light, reflection and hazy evanescence.

The galleries are generous glazed boxes that can accommodate exhibitions and performances. A trio of glass-wall climber-lifts cruise up and down the rear elevation, affording memorable views of the surrounding neighbourhood; the vertiginous escape stairs are similarly articulated on the side elevations. A roof-top terrace café adds to the building's urbane, civilized air.

Fourth-floor plan

1 Entrance
2 Galleries
3 External escape stairs
4 Wall-climber lifts
5 Offices

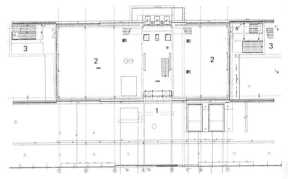

Ground-floor plan
(scale approx. 1:1500)

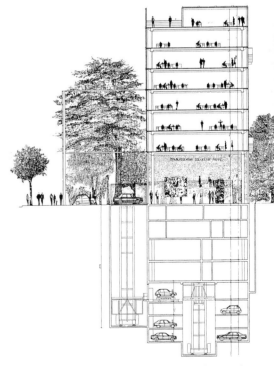

Above Two sheer glass walls project beyond the end of the building, creating an intermediate, indefinable space where the external escape stairs are located. The layering of steel structure and glass wall planes adds tectonic complexity.

Top right Floor plans. The Cartier Foundation's galleries occupy the ground and lower-ground floors. The remaining floors contain a conventional mixture of cellular and open-plan offices.

Right Cross section. Because of building restrictions on the cramped site much of the building is underground. However, the superstructure is dissociated from the substructure; just below ground are a series of heavy beams that transfer loads from the superstructure columns to concrete piles sunk on either side of the basement.

Cross section

Glass Hall

Von Gerkan Marg and Partners, Ian Ritchie Architects

Leipzig, Germany

1995

Top Detail of the glazing system. The huge vault is covered in five thousand identical glass panels, each measuring 3.1 x 1.55 metres, held in place by 'frog finger' fixings attached to cast-steel arms.

Above The shimmering centrepiece of Leipzig's new trade fair park, the glass hall took only eleven months to erect.

Opposite Part of the great glazed flank of the vault. The curving lattice shell is supported by a series of arched steel trusses. Diagonal outriggers add longitudinal stiffening and help to stabilize the shell.

Leipzig, in eastern Germany, has been a commercial and trading centre since the Middle Ages. Located on the city's northern edge, the Neue Messe is a monumental expression of commercial and architectural bravado, a striking symbol of the city's post-Communist revitalization. With a proposal that deftly marshals the sprawling programme into a symmetrical setting organized around a landscaped axial valley and flanked by a succession of huge exhibition pavilions, the Hamburg-based practice of von Gerkan Marg and Partners won a limited competition to masterplan the site and design a number of individual buildings.

The centrepiece of the vast 272,000-square-metre park is the Glass Hall, designed in collaboration with London-based architect Ian Ritchie. Since Joseph Paxton daringly exploited the potential of iron-and-glass structures in his Crystal Palace, the glazed vault has become one of the great archetypes of the last 150 years. In the Leipzig hall it attains a new degree of transparency and elegance, combined with remarkable detailing. Because the architects' aim was to provide a central circulation fulcrum through which all visitors would pass on their way to other parts of the site, the building had to be organizationally legible and functionally flexible, capable of housing a wide range of events. Moreover, as the first point of contact for visitors, the hall had to make the right impression, a symbolic embodiment of progress and efficiency.

These intentions have been spectacularly fulfilled. The Glass Hall is a stunning cathedral of light, 243 metres long and 79 metres wide, that can hold thirty thousand people – the largest steel-and-glass structure in Europe (although it is still only half the size of the Crystal Palace). From the inside, the hall appears to be a seamless vaulted glass membrane, weightless and infinite. Its construction is simple but ingenious: ten arched trusses of triangular cross section span the entire width of the hall at 25-metre intervals; attached to them is a square tubular grid that forms a curved lattice shell, with 'frog finger' suction-point fixings that hold over five thousand glazing panels in position. The panels are all a standard size, in contrast to Nicholas Grimshaw's train shed at Waterloo Station (page 136), which uses a similar structural system, but has to accommodate a curve in two directions.

The objective of the Glass Hall's environmental strategy is to generate a modified external climate that never falls below 8° Celsius. In winter the temperature is raised by underfloor heating coils, but the hall is intended to be a partly exterior space, emphasized by such outdoor elements as magnolia trees and stone paving. In summer the coils circulate cold water for cooling, but the main means of temperature reduction is by natural ventilation: the crown of the vault opens, as do panels at lower level, to encourage higher ventilation rates. Protection against overheating is provided by fritting the glazing above the normal view lines on the south side.

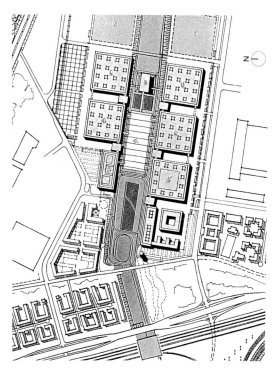

Site plan

Left The axial plan allows for expansion as the site grows. The glass hall is located in a landscaped allée, between the massive trade fair halls, that unites the various exhibition and conference facilities.

Below Inside the cavernous vault. The great archetype of the nineteenth-century glass hall is spectacularly reinterpreted using contemporary technologies of nodal fixing and silicone jointing. Suspending the glass skin from an external structure has resulted in an exquisitely seamless interior. Ceramic banding on the glass gives protection from heat build-up.

Opposite, top The cross section reveals how the glass hall is connected to surrounding buildings by a series of glazed bridges that penetrate the vault.

Opposite, middle and bottom Long section and plan of lower entrance level. The hall orientates and directs visitors to other parts of the site. The glass bridges connect with stone-clad plinths at upper level. Underneath the plinths at lower level are ancillary facilities such as restaurants, information points and lavatories. Lines of magnolia trees create a formal landscaped courtyard.

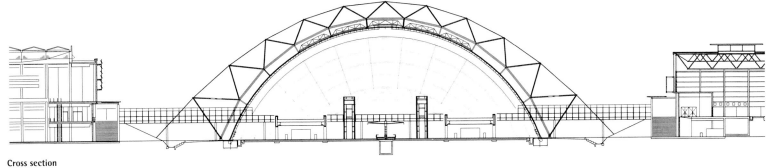

Cross section

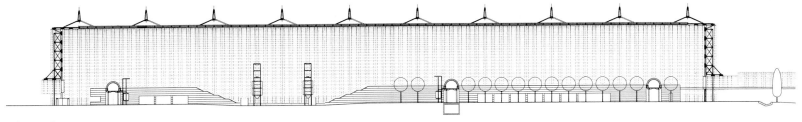

Long section

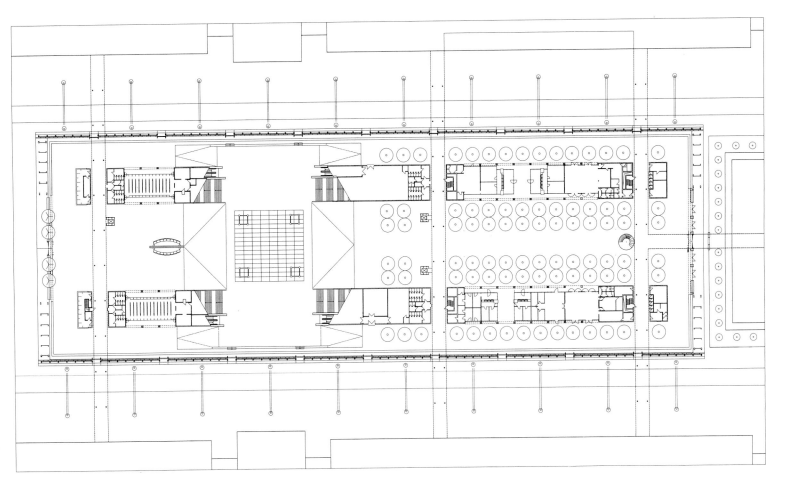

Plan of lower entrance level (scale approx. 1:1250)

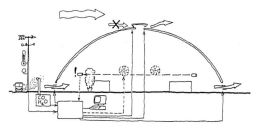

Diagram showing principles of environmental control

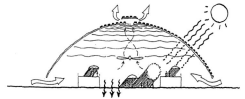

Summer

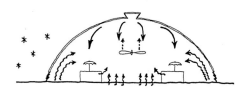

Winter

Left top Three diagrams demonstrating the principles of environmental control. In summer cooling is achieved through assisted natural ventilation, local shading, cooling floor and fritted glass. In winter, convector heating at the edges and the heated floor keep temperatures above 8C°.

Left middle Detail of the cast-steel arm that connects the panes of glass to the tubular lattice structure.

Left bottom The isometric of the vault shows the relationship between the various structural and constructional elements.

Right Part of the self-supporting end walls, which were conceived as a series of concentric arched trusses. The end walls had to be self-supporting because the skin of the vault could not accommodate any further horizontal wind loads without serious risk of deformation.

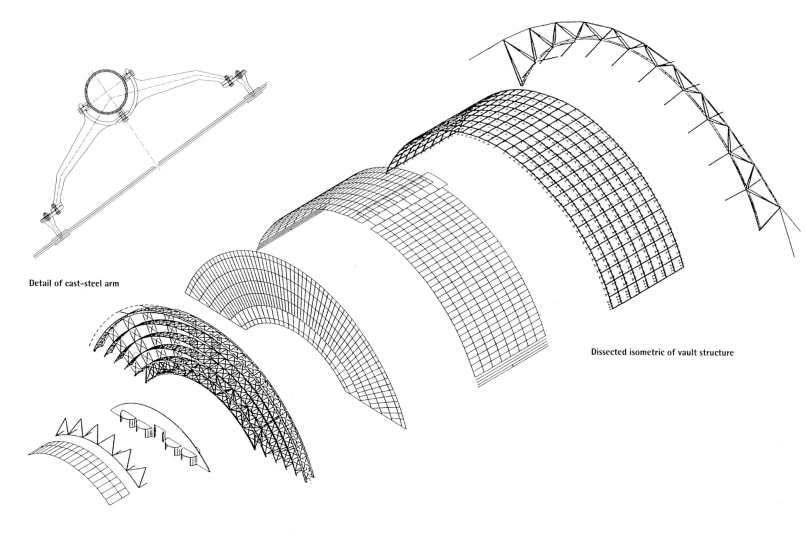

Detail of cast-steel arm

Dissected isometric of vault structure

Energy Matters

Inland Revenue Headquarters in Nottingham,
by Michael Hopkins and Partners (page 98)

Cité Internationale

- Renzo Piano Building Workshop
- Lyons, France
- 1995

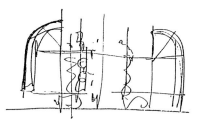

Top South elevation of the office blocks. Homogeneous terra-cotta cladding combined with a selectively applied glazed outer skin unifies the different heights and functions of the blocks that make up the Cité Internationale complex. The curved top of the glazed skin recalls the nineteenth-century greenhouses in the adjacent Parc de la Tête d'Or.

Above Piano's evocative initial sketch shows the genesis of the curved form.

Opposite One of the bridges that bisects the main pedestrian mall and connects with a new boulevard that runs along the edge of the River Rhône.

As France's second largest city, Lyons is the political, cultural and social fulcrum of the Rhône-Alpes region and internationally important as a trade centre between Milan, Barcelona and Zurich. During the 1980s, the city launched 'Lyons 2010', an ambitious urban development plan intended to recast its stolid bourgeois image into something more progressive and dynamic.

A competition was held in 1985 for the redevelopment of the Foire International de Lyon, a group of exhibition and trade fair buildings that date back to 1918 and situated on the River Rhône, adjoining the nineteenth-century Parc de la Tête d'Or. Renzo Piano's winning scheme initially proposed linking the original buildings with a curving pedestrian mall, but because this was considered commercially unviable, all the existing blocks except one were demolished and Piano was commissioned to produce a revised design.

A mixture of offices, cultural facilities, shops, dwellings and a conference centre, the Cité Internationale is meant to be a city in microcosm, a place where people will live and work, not just another retail or business ghetto. The project reflects Piano's concern with urban place-making, energy use and connecting with nature. Here he transplants the messy vitality of the city into a monumental covered street that follows the gently curving path of the Rhône and is flanked by a double row of free-standing pavilions. The scheme meshes firmly with its surroundings, which, despite the city centre's proximity, are neither urban nor suburban. The main entrance faces the river and is reached by a new urban boulevard designed by landscape architect Michel Corajoud. A tree-lined promenade on the park side serves as a secondary route, and numerous connecting side streets make the complex flexible and easy to penetrate, like the labyrinthine *traboules* that wind between buildings in the older parts of Lyons.

The first of three construction phases of the huge scheme is complete; the initial building contains a conference centre, a pair of office blocks, a cinema and the conversion of the original entrance pavilion into a contemporary art museum. The differing heights, functions and fenestration of the blocks are unified by crisp terra-cotta cladding, which weathers well and imparts a warm grainy texture to the walls. The terra cotta's robustness contrasts with areas of unframed glass panels that project from the façades, shimmering and dematerializing in a manner that Piano has described as pointillist. The outer skin of glazing improves the buildings' energy efficiency while intercepting the force of the wind and the rain, so that the conventional windows behind can always be open. Thus in summer the buildings can be naturally ventilated, and in winter the glass traps heat behind it, acting as another layer of insulation. On the taller blocks, the curved glass skin subtly alludes to the barrel vaults of the nineteenth-century greenhouses in the Parc de la Tête d'Or.

Perspective of the internal street

Left A perspective of the internal street, which was conceived as a dense, multi-use precinct intended to nurture the diversity and vitality of the city.

Above The first phase of the Cité consists of a conference centre, office and art gallery. These will be added to incrementally to form a serpentine block following along the edge of the River Rhône.

Below A detail of the external glazed skin, which provides a barrier to wind and rain so that windows behind can be opened, encouraging natural ventilation. The glazing system also helps to trap and store heat in the winter and cool the building in the summer.

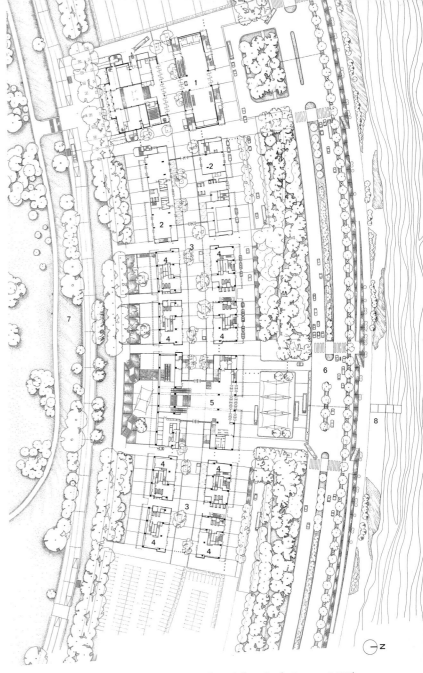

Ground-floor plan (scale approx. 1:1875)

Left The internal street, with shops, offices and cultural activities enlivening the space at ground level. The robust detailing and use of unadorned materials – steel, glass and terra cotta – is an antidote to the typically characterless pedestrian mall.

Above The ground-floor plan of the first phase shows the relationship of the Cité to the river and park.

1 Contemporary art museum
2 Hotel
3 Internal street
4 Offices
5 Conference centre
6 Riverside boulevard
7 Parc de la Tête d'Or
8 River Rhône

UNESCO Laboratory and Workshop

- Renzo Piano Building Workshop
- Vesima, Italy
- 1991

Above A funicular from the road below provides access to the workshop. A converted adjoining farmhouse is also part of the scheme.

Below The spectacular hillside site, with views over the Gulf of Genoa. The building seems sublimely at one with nature. The translucent roof oversails to protect the entrance.

This purpose-built studio at Vesima, some twenty kilometres west of Genoa, is possibly the most fascinating of Renzo Piano's 'family' of workplaces. It is a laboratory shared by Building Workshop and UNESCO and is used for research into the construction applications of natural materials; for example, the investigation of the structural potential of plant and vegetable fibres and the development of multilayered claddings that could contribute to lower energy consumption in buildings. Piano's consistently innovative synthesis of man-made technology and the natural world is informed by research undertaken in the Vesima laboratory.

Teeteringly poised on a lush hillside overlooking the

Gulf of Genoa, the building gives the appearance of a delicately transparent greenhouse – research specimens are actually grown in the building and its environs, so the horticultural typology is appropriate. The form also alludes to local agricultural greenhouses, a factor that helped to obtain permission to build on this prominent coastal site. Enclosed by a great sloping glass roof, the building is divided into five broad terraces that step down the hillside, merging with the landscape and constantly animated by the vibrant play of the intense Mediterranean light. The interior is a magnificently orchestrated fusion of sunlight, dazzling views and greenery. At the top of the slope, the glazed volume is linked to a small renovated farmhouse which serves as an annexe, reading room and guest house. A funicular – a minimal glass box – transports staff and visitors up from the coast road below.

The farmhouse's solid pink stucco walls contrast with the transparency and lightness of the workshop building. The tectonic elegance of the sloping, oversailing roof is grounded by the warmth and sturdiness of the laminated roof timber in the interior. The roof is clad with double-glazed units, which are shaded by an automatically adjustable system of louvres to avoid overheating.

The building's form has the potential to act as a test bed for prototypes of energy-saving construction currently being developed in the course of Piano's research. For now, it stands as suitable testimony to a 'gentle accommodation' between technology and nature.

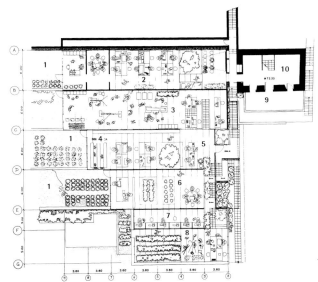

Floor plan (scale approx 1:500)

1 Gardens
2 Education
3 Timber and stone workshop
4 Library
5 Reception
6 Bamboo plants
7 Computer laboratory
8 Natural fibres workshop
9 Terrace
10 Kitchen

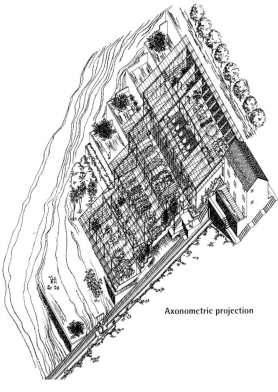

Axonometric projection

Top left Floor plan showing the various research and workshop facilities.

Above Axonometric projection. Based on the local typology of the horticultural greenhouse, the building is conceived as a series of broad terraces that step down the steep hillside.

Left The workshop is not only a magical synthesis of space and light, but an inspired integration of technology with nature that exemplifies Piano's current approach and ideals. Research undertaken in the workshop is applied to a broad range of projects.

Exhibition Hall

- Thomas Herzog
- Hanover, Germany
- 1996

Above The dynamic, wave-profile roof makes a bold architectural statement. It was the tensile roof structure together with a requirement for energy-saving environmental control systems that determined the choice of form.

Opposite The massive, convex 'bellies' of the undulating roof dominate the cavernous interior; the hall measures 220 x 115 metres. Although essentially a neutral volume, the interior is infused with a structural lightness and material transparency. An increased sense of environmental responsibility is giving rise to a new generation of glass halls that exploit new cladding and environmental control technologies.

Hanover's trade fair site is the biggest permanent exposition site in the world. From relatively humble origins as an export fair site contained within the production halls of a former armaments factory, it now approaches the status of a small town, encompassing twenty-six exhibition halls and fifty thousand parking spaces. It is also the location for Expo 2000, the first time an existing trade fair site has been selected for such an event. Not surprisingly, the prospect of the millennial Expo circus coming to Hanover sparked off plans for an ambitious make-over, involving new pavilions and infrastructural improvements.

Thomas Herzog's Hall 26 sets the standard for Hanover's future development. The building is immediately identifiable by a flamboyant silhouette of three gently cresting waves, a commonplace element of industrial vernacular transformed into sensuous undulations that soar up to twenty-nine metres high. The serrations are structured by three rows of pin-jointed steel-trestle masts resembling pylons, which powerfully animate the hangar-like interior.

The vast space can be adapted to suit different exhibition configurations, from streets of individual stands to more irregular, free-form arrangements. The roof's convex 'bellies' diffuse both natural and artificial light, instilling the building with a striking luminosity and prompting comparisons with Paxton's Crystal Palace, the typological progenitor of the trade fair hall. Ancillary facilities are housed in six hermetic pods placed at intervals around the hall perimeter and clad in horizontal timber boarding (similar to Herzog's earlier Wilkahn factory, page 42). Protruding from the glazed skin, the rectangular pods' warmth and tactility are an unexpected foil to the building's sleekness and transparency.

Though essentially a large neutral volume, Hall 26 is distinguished by the architect's consistently innovative approach to structure and servicing. The cost of mechanical ventilation, for example, was greatly reduced by exploiting the principles of natural thermal movement. In summer fresh air is introduced from glass ducts set about four metres above the floor (the constant heavy traffic and shifting of displays mitigates against floor-level outlets). The cool air drops down, then rises as it heats up with the warmth of people and machines; it is finally expelled through the three roof peaks, and any back-flow of air into the hall is prevented by adjustable flaps on the ridges, which can be oriented according to wind direction. In winter, pre-warmed air is directed through long-range nozzles attached to the ducts.

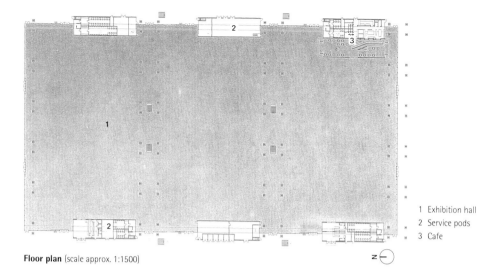

1 Exhibition hall
2 Service pods
3 Cafe

Floor plan (scale approx. 1:1500)

z

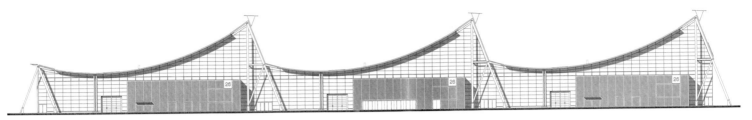

East elevation

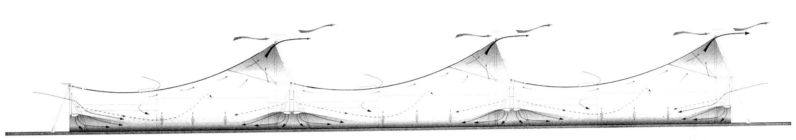

Long section showing environmental control principles

Opposite, above The ground-floor plan delineates the massive 'omniplatz', with services housed in self-contained pods arranged along the perimeter.

Opposite, below The roof peaks are sculptural abstractions of traditional north lights used in factories and warehouses. The rustic timber cladding of the extruded service pods contrasts with the glazed walls.

Above East elevation and long section highlighting the principles of environmental control. Natural thermal movement is exploited, cutting the cost of mechanical ventilation by half. Air is introduced by means of elevated ducts; it drops down and circulates, becomes warm, rises up through the hall and is expelled by vents along the ridges.

Below Isometric of the building structure. The convex roofs are supported by trestle-like masts that demarcate circulation zones within the hall.

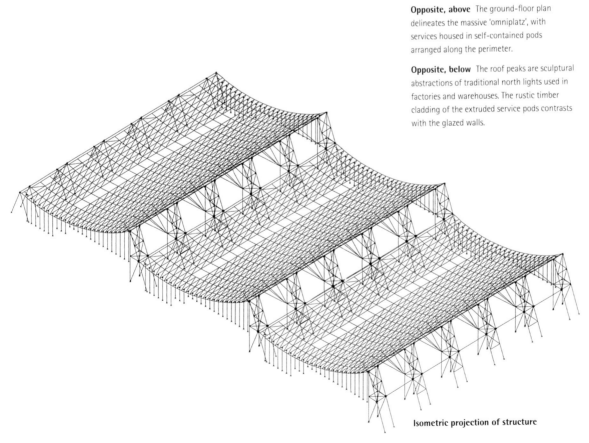

Isometric projection of structure

British Pavilion

- Nicholas Grimshaw and Partners
- Seville, Spain
- 1992

Above Detail of the S-shaped, sail-like louvres and the glistening water wall. The louvres contain solar panels and protect the sheet-metal roof from the sun; they also power the water wall.

Opposite Boat-building technology is appropriated to create the billowing north and south walls of the pavilion. Membranes of PVC-coated polyethylene fabric are stretched between bow-shaped, circular section steel members and attached by means of luff grooves in the same way that sails of yachts are fixed to their masts.

From Paxton's Crystal Palace at the Great Exhibition of 1851 to Aalto's Finnish Pavilion for the 1939 New York World's Fair, expositions have often been the catalysts for visionary architecture. Freedom from the usual constraints can inspire sophisticated and memorable expressions of national identity, although genuine innovation is sometimes overwhelmed by a prevailing tide of kitsch.

Exemplifying this paradox, the 1992 Expo, held in Seville during Spain's recent *annus mirabilis*, turned out to be a vast and occasionally indigestible architectural curate's egg. Surpassing all previous participation records, 110 national pavilions jostled for position on the Isla de la Cartuja in a bizarre, interminable fairground. Within this unforgiving context, Nicholas Grimshaw's British Pavilion was one of the more rewarding attractions.
Few architects were bold enough to develop the Expo's themes of discovery and technological innovation beyond predictable cultural window dressing, but Grimshaw turned his building into a paradigm of environmental experimentation, proving that ecological concerns and High-Tech architecture are not mutually exclusive.

Seville is the hottest city in Europe, with temperatures often reaching 45 degrees Celsius during the summer. To control the effects of climate in hot countries heavy masonry construction is traditionally used, but the temporary nature of Expo pavilions implied a lightweight, demountable structure. Instead of using thermal mass as

an environmental regulator (in the way that Michael Hopkins did at the Inland Revenue, page 98), Grimshaw's steel-and-glass pavilion is a direct and often sensual expression of a range of cooling devices.

The most audacious of these is a giant water wall on the main, east elevation. Developed in collaboration with water sculptor William Pye, sheets of water ripple provocatively down the glazed wall into a pool, which forms a moat around the pavilion. As the Moors of Andalucia understood so well, the presence of running water has an instant physical and psychological cooling effect. Energy to operate the system of water pumps is generated by solar panels mounted on a phalanx of S-shaped roof shades that resemble scaled-down sails.

The yachting analogies continue on the two end walls, where Grimshaw appropriated boat-building technology to construct the poetically nautical arrangement of bow-string trusses and translucent membranes. On the west façade, the side most vulnerable to overheating, Grimshaw devised his own version of thermal mass using shipping containers filled with water. Like all the other building components, they were fabricated in Britain and transported to Seville.

Inside, a system of travelators zigzagging lazily up the inside of the water wall takes visitors around the various exhibition pods and decks. The quality of the internal displays (not executed by Grimshaw), however, failed to match the fascination of the building that housed them.

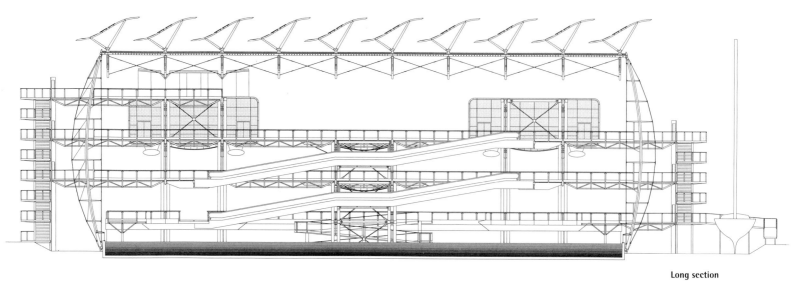

Long section

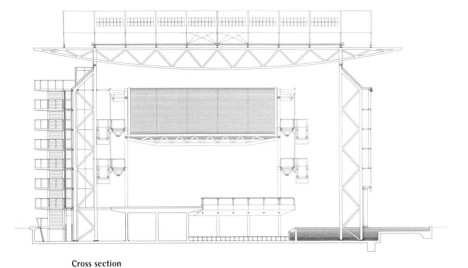

Cross section

1 Concourse
2 Ramp down to courtyard
3 Up travelator
4 Down travelator
5 Entrance bridge
6 Exit ramp
7 Canopy
8 Pool
9 Container wall

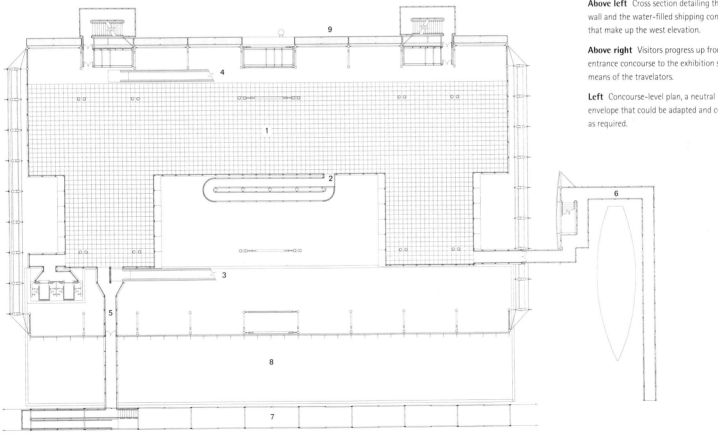

Upper-level plan (scale approx. 1:800)

Opposite, above Long section showing the zig-zagging travelators that connect the exhibition spaces.

Opposite, below The pavilion affirms the environmentally benign potential of technology. The shading and cooling devices give the structure a festive air.

Above left Cross section detailing the water wall and the water-filled shipping containers that make up the west elevation.

Above right Visitors progress up from the entrance concourse to the exhibition spaces by means of the travelators.

Left Concourse-level plan, a neutral envelope that could be adapted and colonized as required.

Microelectronics Park

- Foster and Partners
- Duisburg, Germany
- 1996

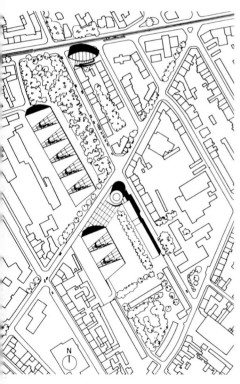

Site plan   **Top**   Detail of the sleek glazed membrane of the Telematic Centre.

Above   The three buildings are located in a new public park.

Opposite   The dramatic circular atrium at the heart of the Telematic Centre.

For over a century the mighty steel and coal industries of the Germany's Ruhr region determined its economic development. In a pattern repeated across Europe, the factories, mines and social structures that once powered the muscle of heavy industry are now decaying or obsolescent. The new microelectronics park in the northern German city of Duisburg is a bold attempt to revitalize a region that once depended on these industries but is now radically reshaping its industrial landscape. Aiming to become one of the most significant microelectronics locations in Europe, the Duisburg complex will employ some three thousand people, primarily in research and development.

The site lies in the Neudorf district, midway between the city centre and the town's university. The complex comprises three buildings loosely linked by a swathe of parkland. The most prominent element on the site is the Business Promotion Centre, which marks the park's entrance and acts as a landmark on the city-university axis. Based on a lens-shaped plan, the structure is a sharp crystalline sliver, spare and finely honed. Its curved roof drops from eight to five storeys, reinforcing its sculptural quality. Cellular offices are arranged around an elliptical core, with meeting spaces in the prows. A highly sophisticated building management system analyzes current and anticipated weather conditions to calculate the optimum levels of heating, cooling and shading, and by adjusting horizontal lattice blinds in the triple-glazed

external skin, occupants can fine-tune the temperature and light in their own spaces. The responsiveness of the system sets new standards for environmental control.

The second building in the complex is the Telematic Centre, located on the corner of two residential streets to the southeast of the Business Promotion Centre. The truncated cylindrical volume is connected to an existing technology transfer centre and contains facilities for seminars, events and exhibitions. Five floors of offices are organized around a generous circular atrium that descends through two underground storeys to swell out into an exhibition space surrounded by workshops and conference rooms. The public focus of the building is the airy, luminous volume of the atrium.

The recently completed Microelectronics Centre, the third element in the complex, consists of three wedge-shaped 'fingers' of offices, laboratories and workshops linked by two internal courtyards. The entire five-story building is enclosed by a curved roof, which is intermittently glazed where it spans the courtyards. The building's quadrant-shaped profile recalls the form of the Law Faculty at Cambridge (page 54).

All three buildings epitomize Foster's capacity for sleek form-making coupled with a precise handling of materials and detailing. The quiet refinement of the architecture is reinforced by sophisticated environmental-control strategies that reflect the architect's wider ongoing concern with energy use.

1 Atrium
2 Cellular offices
3 Existing technology transfer centre

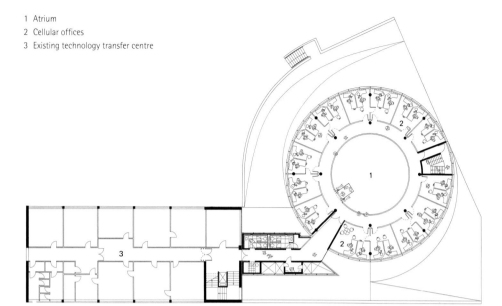

Left Ground-floor plan of the Telematic Centre. The new building is linked to an existing technology transfer centre. Cellular offices are organized around the circular atrium.

Below Cross section through the truncated cylindrical volume of the Telematic Centre. A spiralling ramp leads down into a basement exhibition space.

Telematic Centre lower–ground–floor plan (scale approx. 1:500)

Telematic Centre cross section

Below Diagram illustrating the Business Promotion Centre's environmental control system. The external walls are triple glazed and feature an intermediate layer of adjustable blinds. A transparent inner skin of insulation moderates extreme temperatures. Local radiant heat gains, from both machine and occupants, are exploited. An 'intelligent' building-management system predicts heating and cooling demands and responds accordingly.

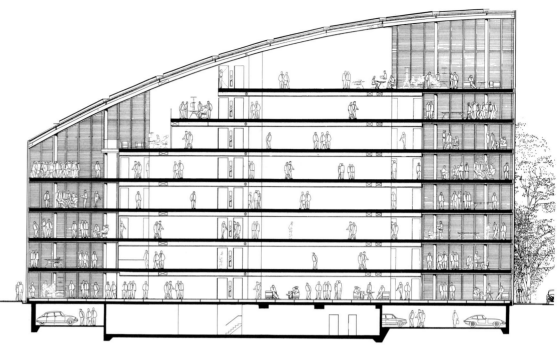

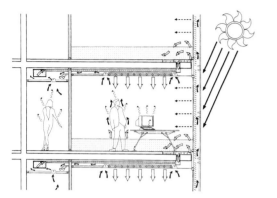

Business Promotion Centre climate control scheme

Business Promotion Centre long section

Right Long section and plan of the Business Promotion Centre. The lens-shaped plan contains cellular offices around its perimeter and meeting rooms in the pointed ends.

Below By combining a level of environmental control with a seamless glass skin, Foster has effectively created a highly sophisticated modern version of Le Corbusier's *mur neutralisant*.

Below right Detail of the prow-like end. By using a bolt-fixing system, the joints between the glazed panels can be reduced to the width of a silicone seal, heightening the transparency of the exterior.

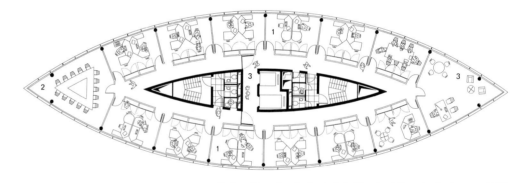

Business Promotion Centre typical office–level floor plan (scale approx. 1:500)

1 Cellular offices
2 Meeting rooms
3 Circulation core

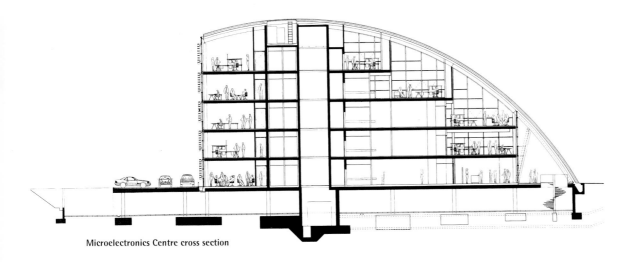

Microelectronics Centre cross section

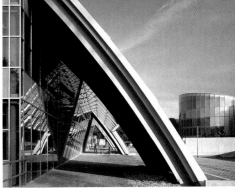

Above The vaulted structure of the Microelectronics Centre is exposed, creating an arcade-like promenade. The cylindrical form of the Telematic Centre is visible in the distance.

Below One of the atria between the offices – an exploration of the typology of the glass hall – acts as an intermediate indoor/outdoor space.

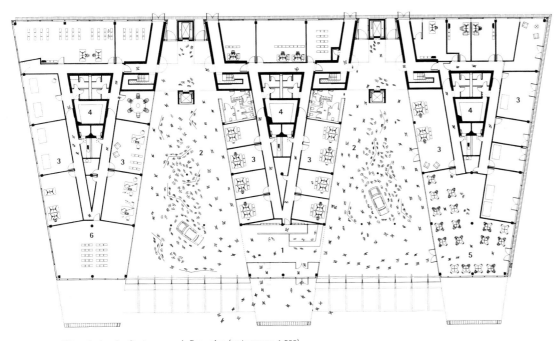

Microelectronics Centre ground–floor plan (scale approx. 1:500)

1 Entrance hall
2 Atrium
3 Office units
4 Circulation and service cores
5 Cafe
6 Lecture theatre

Opposite Detail of the west elevation of the Microelectronics Centre. The external envelope uses transparent insulation material, sun reflectors and heat collectors to create the optimum temperature balance and gain according to outside climate conditions.

Top Cross section through one of the office 'fingers' in the Microelectronics Centre.

Above Ground-floor plan of the Microelectronics Centre. Like the Telematic Centre, it contains facilities for the start-up of small- and medium-sized new companies. The two atria between the office wedges can be used for a number of public and semi-public activities.

Inland Revenue Headquarters

- Michael Hopkins and Partners
- Nottingham, England
- 1995

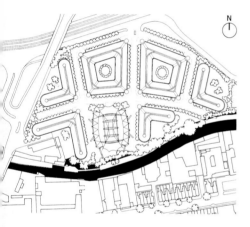

Site plan

Top The tented structure of the staff amenity complex is a signature Hopkins device. Here the billowing peaks house all the non-administrative functions. Its lightness and translucence contrast with the robust quality of the offices.

Above The site plan shows how the pattern of streets and gardens reflects the surrounding urban texture. Offices are housed in a mixture of courtyard and L-shaped blocks.

Opposite The rounded ends of two of the L-shaped office blocks. The repetitive rhythm of structural brick bays recalls the functional tradition of Nottingham's nineteenth-century warehouses.

The new headquarters for the Inland Revenue occupies a former industrial site on a canal in the centre of Nottingham, within sight of Nottingham Castle.

Hopkins's scheme deftly dismantles the massive 400,000-square-foot complex into seven discrete buildings arrayed in a series of radiating bands of streets, gardens and courtyards along a tree-lined boulevard that extends across the site in a gentle arc, terminating at the canal towpath on the western edge. The density of the development takes its cue from the urban fabric immediately to the north. The character of the individual buildings, with their rhythmic red-brick piers and lead-clad roofs, is redolent of Nottingham's nineteenth-century industrial warehouses, archaeological fragments of which can still be found along the canal's edges.

The Inland Revenue buildings, however, are thoroughly modern hives of industry. The 3.2-metre width of the façade module, which articulates and defines the elevations, is based on the frontage of a typical cellular office. Service cores are located at the end of each office wing, adjacent to cylindrical glass-block stair towers. The widths of both the standard floors (13.8 metres) and the overhanging upper storeys (16 metres) coordinate precisely with European furniture modules.

The exception to the solidity and rigour of the red-brick buildings is the tented amenity block, which contains a sports hall, gym, nursery, staff restaurant and bar. Its sensual meringue peaks, held in place by a filigree of cable stays, recall the Mound Stand and research laboratories for Schlumberger (completed in 1987 and 1984).

Perhaps the most innovative aspect of the Inland Revenue programme, however, is its enlightened environmental-control strategy. In a rare public sector commitment to green values, the architects designed the buildings to modify the environment with minimal recourse to mechanical systems: the offices are naturally ventilated and in summer the building fabric is used as a heat store, which can absorb heat during the day and be cooled by drawing air into the building at night. In warm weather the glazed stair towers also function as thermal chimneys, drawing external air through the offices; the structural piers, which were built off site, are made of dense, semi-engineering Nottingham bricks, which, with the concrete ceiling vaults, act as a thermal flywheel that maintains an equable internal climate. Even though the structures are as thermally massive as possible to maximize ambient energy use, the tight construction schedule meant that much of the construction was prefabricated, yet the reliance on off-site construction does not compromise the buildings' tectonic quality.

The Inland Revenue complex could have been an oppressive, bureaucratic anthill. Instead, through the campus-like scale and organization of the buildings, it gives its workers a sense of identity and community as well as a measure of control over their environment.

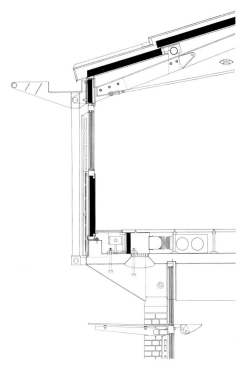

Detailed section through attic wall

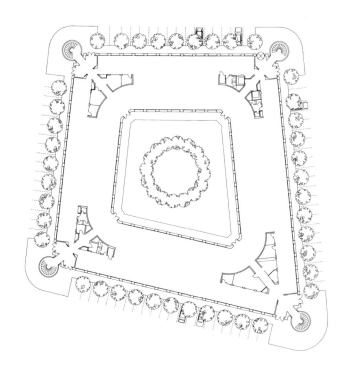

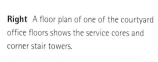

Right A floor plan of one of the courtyard office floors shows the service cores and corner stair towers.

Below From this elevated vantage point the campus-like scale and layout of the complex are apparent. The tented peaks of the amenity block create a bold new civic landmark.

Typical office-floor plan (scale approx. 1:1000)

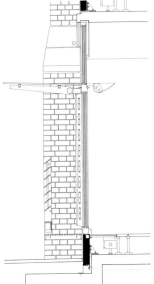

Detailed section through foot of bay

Above Detailed sections through a typical external wall show the precast brick piers used to support precast concrete vaults, which reduce in size as the storey height increases. The combination of brick and concrete gives the building a high thermal mass that is exploited in the environmental control system.

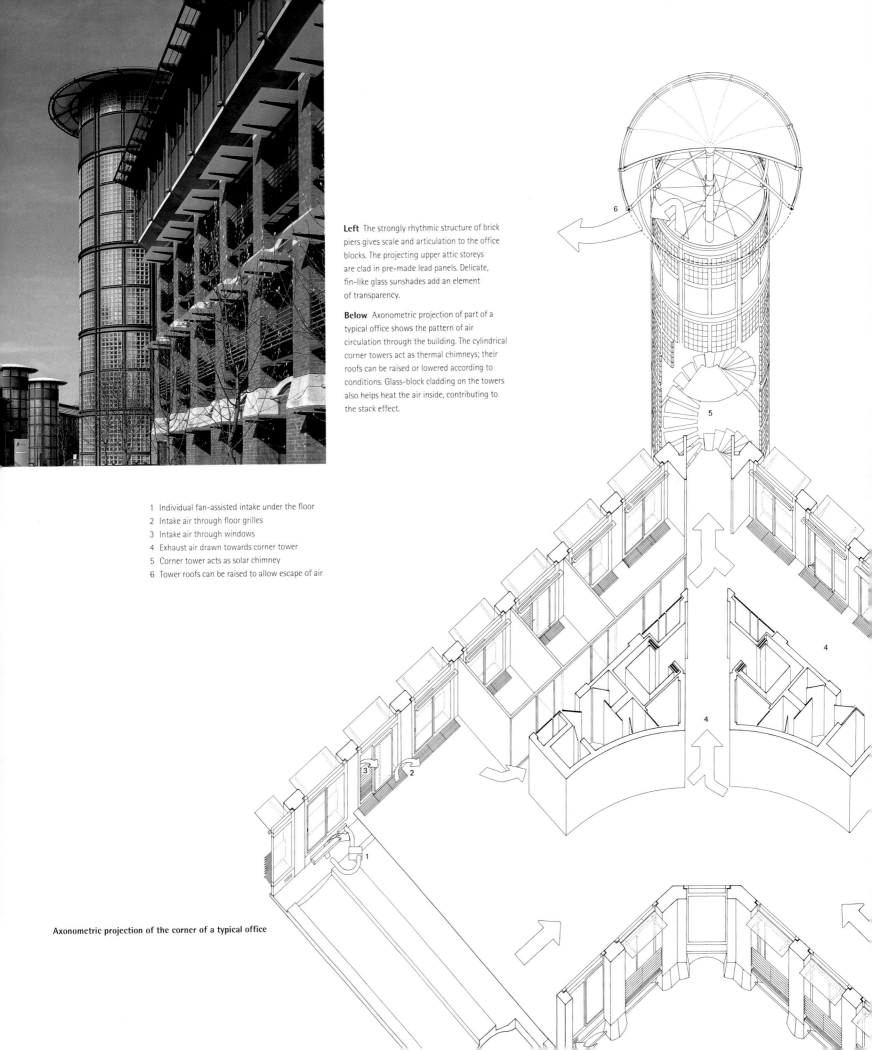

Left The strongly rhythmic structure of brick piers gives scale and articulation to the office blocks. The projecting upper attic storeys are clad in pre-made lead panels. Delicate, fin-like glass sunshades add an element of transparency.

Below Axonometric projection of part of a typical office shows the pattern of air circulation through the building. The cylindrical corner towers act as thermal chimneys; their roofs can be raised or lowered according to conditions. Glass-block cladding on the towers also helps heat the air inside, contributing to the stack effect.

1 Individual fan-assisted intake under the floor
2 Intake air through floor grilles
3 Intake air through windows
4 Exhaust air drawn towards corner tower
5 Corner tower acts as solar chimney
6 Tower roofs can be raised to allow escape of air

Axonometric projection of the corner of a typical office

Urban Responses

Genoa's revitalized Porto Vecchio by
Renzo Piano Building Workshop (page 120)

Channel Four Headquarters

- Richard Rogers Partnership
- London, England
- 1994

Top Scuttling pods of glazed wall-climber lifts enliven the exterior.

Above The tall, curving atrium. Circular glass lenses set into the floors of the galleries enhance the sense of transparency.

Opposite From the entrance bridge, protected by its perilously suspended canopy, the tectonic and spatial drama of the building unfolds.

Since its inception in the early 1980s, independent-television company Channel 4 occupied a disparate collection of buildings in central London. By 1990 the company had decided to consolidate its television studios, post-production facilities and offices in one complex, so a limited competition was held to find a suitable design. Richard Rogers Partnership won with a scheme that makes a provocative architectural statement in a part of London dominated by dull civil-service offices and nondescript mansion blocks, yet within reach of Westminster Abbey and the Houses of Parliament.

A deliberate set-piece of urban theatre, the building exploits its tight site by means of a relatively simple plan: two four-storey wings containing offices above ground and studios below are joined together at right angles by a knuckle of circulation. Their union is consummated by a concave glass wall, dramatically suspended from a delicate network of stainless-steel rods and cables. Terminating either end of the piazzalike space created by the corner's recess are sentinel towers, which contain lifts and meeting rooms and are topped with bristling satellite dishes and plant machinery.

A glazed, umbilical bridge leads up to the main entrance, but not before crossing a circular moat with unexpected views through an oculus of the preview theatre's foyer below. With its tiers of cantilevered walkways and steel roof structure (all primary steelwork is painted a reddish brown, apparently the precise colour of San Francisco's Golden Gate Bridge), the four-storey main entrance atrium forms the building's spectacular, transparent hub. From here there are glimpses into the staff canteen, half a level down, and through to the tranquil green courtyard at the heart of the complex. On the upper levels, the curved link between the two office wings contains executive suites, some of which face into the atrium, and a directors' terrace on the top floor overlooking the central courtyard.

As at Rogers's Lloyd's Bank (completed in 1986), some of the fixed elements of circulation and servicing are extruded from the central volume. This creates flexible interior spaces and breaks down the scale of the building, using the dissection of its various elements in an almost decorative way – what critic Deyan Sudjic has called 'a paradoxical use of technology for mannerist ends'. It also implants the building firmly into the streetscape by announcing its use and exposing its inner workings through the lift capsules' vertical traffic and the constant human animation of the pivotal atrium – a true expression of Rogers's long-standing concern with making buildings that contribute and respond to the life of the city.

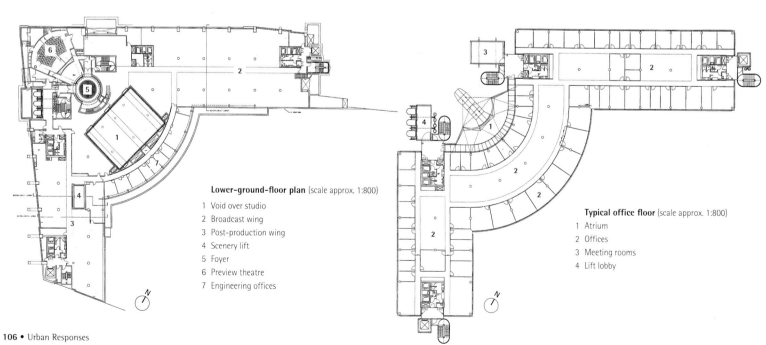

Lower-ground-floor plan (scale approx. 1:800)

1 Void over studio
2 Broadcast wing
3 Post-production wing
4 Scenery lift
5 Foyer
6 Preview theatre
7 Engineering offices

Typical office floor (scale approx. 1:800)

1 Atrium
2 Offices
3 Meeting rooms
4 Lift lobby

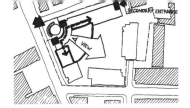

Views and orientation

Opposite, left Framed by bristling sentinel towers and visceral gadgetry, the corner entrance piazza responds generously to the public realm.

Opposite, right The smaller of the two office wings. Here the architectural language is more restrained.

Opposite, below The floor plans show how the two office wings are united by the knuckle of the atrium. Stair towers and meeting rooms are isolated on the edges of the building.

Left The curving link between the two wings. The restaurant terrace at ground level overlooks the courtyard garden to the rear of the building.

Right Generative sketches of the principles of site analysis and development.

Below The cross section shows the direct flow of space through the entrance piazza, atrium, restaurant and garden.

Buildings reinforcing urban pattern

Entrance and communal heart

Section through garden and atrium

1 Void over studio
2 Restaurant
3 Terrace
4 Plant
5 Car parking
6 Atrium
7 Offices
8 Entrance piazza
9 Garden

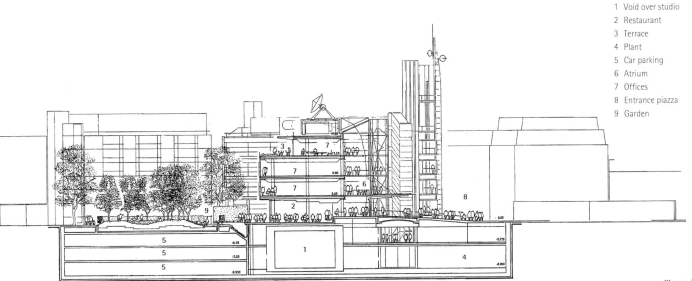

Bracken House

- Michael Hopkins and Partners
- London, England
- 1992

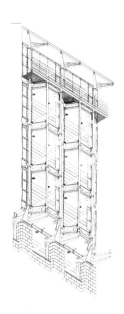

Top Detail of the glass-and-gunmetal oriel window module, a modern reworking of nineteenth-century Oriel Chambers by Peter Ellis in Liverpool.

Above Axonometric projection of the window wall. The three-fingered cantilever brackets that frame the oriel window bays rest on rusticated stone bases.

Opposite An incisive, ice-glass tongued canopy discreetly marks the entrance to the revived City palazzo.

Commissioned by newspaper magnate Brendan Bracken, Albert Richardson's stolid palazzo completed in 1959 lies in the heart of the City, London's financial district, near St Paul's Cathedral. The building was originally the home of the Financial Times, before the paper's journalists were decanted to a nondescript building in Southwark and its print works relocated to more distinguished quarters (designed by Nicholas Grimshaw in 1988) in the Docklands. Appropriately pink – like the Financial Times itself – Bracken House was the first post-war building to attain historic-preservation status when it was given Grade II listing in 1987.

The inspirational and formal model was Guarino Guarini's Baroque Palazzo Carignano in Turin, with its two wings joined together by an elliptical entrance block. Bracken House's original H-shaped plan comprised two office wings buttressing a large octagonal central section that housed the print works. When the building's component functions were dismantled, it was acquired by a Japanese client, Obayashi, who commissioned Michael Hopkins to produce a proposal for redevelopment. The programme called for an intelligent office building capable of accommodating the modern technology on which the City of London has come to depend.

In just thirty years Bracken House was verging on obsolescence but Hopkins's surgical yet sympathetic intervention has spectacularly revived it. The central section was removed and the two book-end office wings

retained. A doughnut-shaped volume of highly serviced offices took the place of the printing hall – ink symbolically superseded by electronics. Bracken House's new engine room is now a large dealing hall on the lower ground floor, the scarcely discernible hum of computers replacing the throb of the presses.

Hopkins's façades provide a sharply articulated foil to Richardson's heroic ends blocks: the faceted oriel configuration of cast-gunmetal cladding, spandrels and support brackets is a modern extemporization on Richardson's basic concertina rhythm. The fluid assemblies bear down through three-fingered cantilever brackets on to pink Hollington stone piers that form the reinvented palazzo's rusticated base, like archaeological fragments of the original building.

Bracken House challenged Hopkins to confront history in a new way, seeking and reinterpreting precedents from nineteenth-century French structural rationalism. The muscular glass-block atrium that dramatically penetrates the doughnut plan evokes comparisons with Henri Labrouste's book stacks in Paris's Bibliothèque Nationale. Less obviously, the complex balletic interaction of thrust and counterthrust in the new building would have been the envy of the most assiduous Gothic Revivalist.

Bracken House is also significant in that it shows Hopkins 'bringing technology to town', away from the green field sites of High Tech's origins. Here, it responds with style and substance to the life of the City.

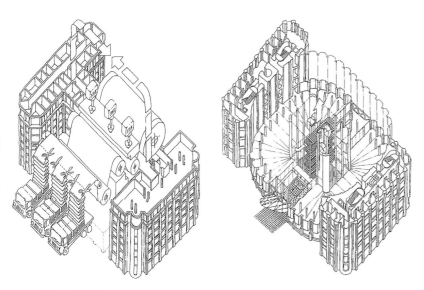

Concept sketches

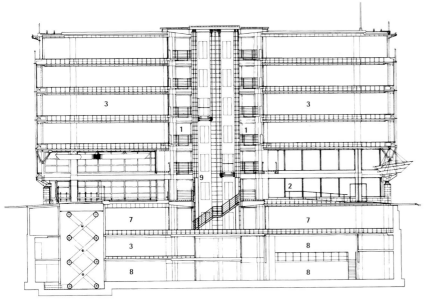

Cross section

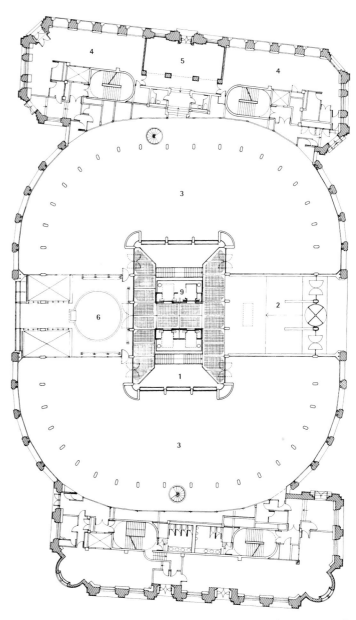

1 Atrium
2 Main entrance
3 New offices
4 Retained office wings
5 Retained entrance hall
6 Loading bay
7 Dealer floor
8 Service area
9 Lift

Ground-floor plan (scale approx. 1:500)

Top Concept sketches reveal how the original relationship of printing hall and office wings has evolved into a modified arrangement of a 'doughnut' of office accommodation inserted between the existing wings.

Above Cross section and ground-floor plan. The new doughnut of office space is organized around a central atrium.

Opposite The tall, hard-edged space of the atrium recalls the structural rationalism of Labrouste. Freestanding steel lift shafts are connected by daylight-filtering, glass-floored bridges.

Kabuki-cho Tower

- Richard Rogers Partnership
- Tokyo, Japan
- 1993

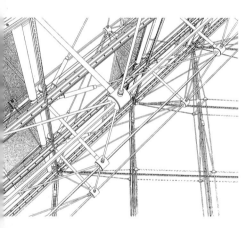

Perspective of glazed atrium roof

Top One of a series of projects for commercial buildings in Japan, the Kabuki-cho Tower was constructed at the height of the economic boom in Tokyo. The lack of aesthetic controls and the stringent anti-earthquake regulations compounded the unorthodox context.

Above Perspective revealing the intricate filigree structure of the glazed atrium roof.

Opposite Detail of the vertiginous fire escape stairs and yellow washroom modules that cling to the side of the building.

A series of projects in Japan has given the Richard Rogers Partnership the opportunity to pursue formal and spatial experiments that would be virtually impossible in the West. Although conforming to the constraints of a standard commercial brief, each project has been used as a vehicle for technical innovation, notably in the area of exposed steelwork. The Kabuki-cho Tower occupies a typically dense and jumbled site – hemmed in between a nondescript modern office block and a traditional Japanese villa with a walled garden – in one of Tokyo's more colourful *yakusa* (gangster)-dominated districts.

Kabuki-cho contains ten storeys of offices, each floor a compact rectangle of maximized lettable space. In a well-rehearsed reprise of a favourite Rogers device, services and circulation cores are pulled out to the building's exterior to articulate its mass. Yellow washroom modules are neatly stacked up like child's blocks, and the perforated-metal escape stair, suspended from the raw-concrete lift tower by a network of stainless-steel rods attached to the outer half landings, is fully exposed (rather terrifyingly for potential users).

Local planning controls stipulated that the building should be situated at the rear of the site, creating a large open area on the street front. This space was hewn out and covered by a sloping glass roof that allows light down to two floors below ground. To make the four-storey-high roof as unobtrusive as possible, so that it appears to float on thin air, the structure is supported by a series of lightweight steel bowstring trusses linked together by tension wires. The deceptive delicacy of the members belies a precisely engineered capability to withstand the extreme loadings periodically generated by local typhoon and seismic activity.

Steel is rarely used in an external structural context in Japan, largely because of stringent national building codes, but also because of an inherent conservatism engendered by the reliance on standard construction packages from off-the-peg suppliers. To achieve the same degree of transparency and lightness by orthodox means would have resulted in a massively oversized and ungainly structure, more suited to an oil rig than a building. As it was, the design required a special dispensation from the Japanese Construction Ministry.

Kabuki-cho's effect is heightened by the expressive potential of structure and materials rigorously and inventively applied. Western architects working in Japan have often been commissioned specifically to produce signature buildings that are predictable exercises in attention-seeking. Here, by intelligently challenging existing convention, Rogers has made an invigorating – and quite possibly pioneering – contribution to the fractured Tokyo cityscape.

Opposite The glazed maw of the six-storey atrium, which brings light down to the lower floors of offices. The deceptively light bowstring trusses are capable of withstanding huge seismic loadings. Integrated within the structure is a sophisticated sun-blind mechanism that diffuses glare. Original project drawings proposed an entrance bridge over the void (shown here in plan and section), which may still be constructed.

Left The tower in the fragmented urban context of Tokyo. The challenge of the highly restricted site gave rise to an experimental, overtly constructional approach.

Below Plans and section show the extremely compact floor plates. To free up as much lettable space as possible, service elements are compressed into perimeter modules.

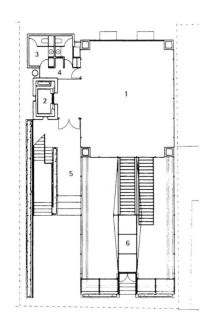

Ground-floor plan (scale appox. 1:500)

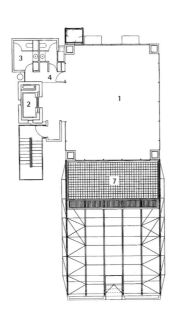

Fifth-floor plan

1 Office
2 Lift
3 WCs
4 Kitchen
5 Escape balcony
6 Future bridge
7 Balcony

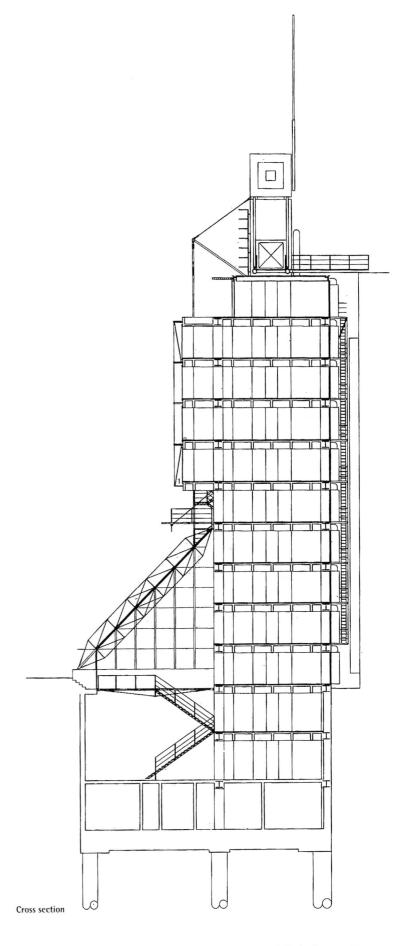

Cross section

Carré d'art

- Foster and Partners
- Nîmes, France
- 1993

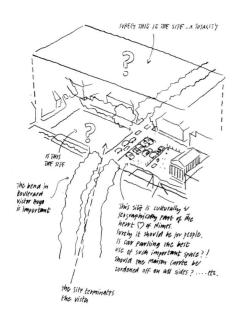

SURELY THIS IS THE SITE - A TOTALITY

?

IS THIS
THE SITE

The bend in
Boulevard
Victor Hugo
is important

This site is culturally &
seographically part of the
heart ♡ of Nimes.
Surely it should be for people.
Is car parking the best
use of such important space?!
Should the Maison Carrée be
cordoned off on all sides?....etc.

The site terminates
the vista

Top Twin temples of Nîmes – Foster's Carré d'art sits cheek by jowl with the ancient Maison Carré. The new intervention fits easily and lightly into the grain of the city.

Above A design development sketch analyzing the site and its context. The relationship of the new building with its historic neighbour is the dominant consideration; the site therefore is treated as a greater urban whole.

Opposite The magical play of Provençal light diffused through the louvred canopy that forms part of the building's portico. The precise quality of the detailing is signature Foster.

Conceived as the 'Pompidou Centre of the South', the Carré d'art in Nîmes is a cultural facility without equal in the region. Yoking together a wide range of activities – library, art gallery, archives, offices and restaurant – it offers multipurpose spaces for contemporary artistic creation, reading, contemplation, documentation and book-lending. The site lies in the very heart of the city, on a plot formerly occupied by a theatre destroyed by fire in 1952.

Inserting any kind of modern building into a delicate historical fabric requires astute sensitivity, but the challenge was compounded by the extreme antiquity of the Maison Carée, the new building's immediate neighbour and one of the best-preserved Roman temples in the world. From the outset the project was thus underscored by a powerful yet invigorating tension between ancient and modern, the result of which is clearly evident in the final built form.

Foster's civic temple of culture is a cool abstraction of its historic neighbour. Like the temple, it has blank side walls and an open front; like the temple, it is framed by a portico, a generous, lightweight louvred canopy for diffusing the harsh Mediterranean light. Instead of Corinthian columns, however, Foster's portico is supported by five obscenely slender steel poles 17 metres high. The glass façades are simple, refined and handsomely proportioned; the exposed structural frame of circular concrete columns is infilled with rectangular

glass panels, some clear, some milkily translucent like Japanese *shoji* (rice paper) screens.

Inside, the various spaces are arranged around a canyonlike atrium, with a big, set-piece glass staircase cascading through the void. At the top of the building is an open-air terrace restaurant, a delightful outdoor room at roof level. From here, visitors can survey the ancient undisturbed grandeur of the 1700-year-old Maison Carré opposite.

The Carré d'art is a signature Foster building, but despite its apparent simplicity it has a concealed, technical intricacy. Like an iceberg, most of the building is beneath the surface, extending down some 20 metres. The five basement levels were formed by perimeter diaphragm walling techniques, and are almost entirely below the surrounding water level. With so little building mass above, a layer has been installed beneath the lowest slab to pump away excess water and avoid the risk of flooding. The fair-faced concrete columns were almost untouched after striking, displaying an impressive uniformity of texture and colour.

The slenderness of the steel columns carrying the louvred entrance canopy is made possible by enlarged foundations, which provide what is effectively a cantilevered support. Grappling with a very complex programme on a constricted, highly sensitive site, Foster shows his mastery of abstraction and neutrality.

Opposite Gently reaching out to embrace the city and provide shelter from the elements, the Carré d'art's slender portico is a modern abstraction of a traditional form. The soaring glass walls allow tantalizing glimpses into the building and a sense of the activity within.

Right A steel-and-glass stair dizzily cascading through an atrium forms the spatial set piece at the heart of the building.

Below Cross section through the site, with the Maison Carré on the right. For all its appearance of transparency and weightlessness, the building has a concealed, subterranean complexity. Five storeys located underground and below the level of the water table necessitated the construction of a perimeter diaphragm wall.

Bottom Ground-floor plan. A double-height entrance hall leads to the drama of the atrium beyond. Conceived as an accessible cultural institution (modelled on the democratic Pompidou Centre), the building possesses a seamlessness and generosity of space that is intended to encourage casual visitors.

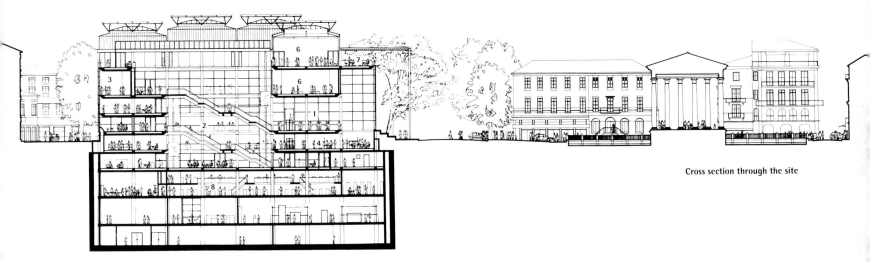

Cross section through the site

1 Entrance hall
2 Atrium
3 Offices
4 Library
5 Exhibition space
6 Galleries
7 Restaurant
8 Archive
9 Bookshop

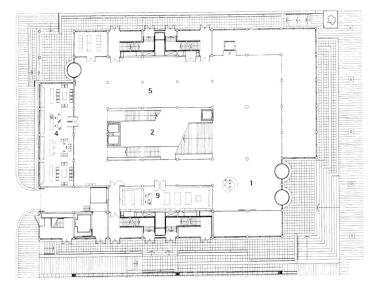

Ground-floor plan (scale approx. 1:500)

Port Restoration

- Renzo Piano Building Workshop
- Genoa, Italy
- 1992

Top The splayed booms of the symbolic, sculptural Bigo dominate Genoa's revitalized Porto Vecchio. In the foreground are the delicately fragmented, multi-sailed wind sculptures designed by Susumu Shingu.

Above Piano's generative sketch shows the harbour and city compressed against the mountains.

Opposite The festive, tented form of the Piazza del Feste (a new event space) has overtones of Archigram's carnivalesque urban projects.

One of the most vibrant port cities in Italy, Genoa has evolved around its great natural harbour. Apart from its economic and trading supremacy, the port has a wider historical significance: in 1492 Christopher Columbus, one of the city's most famous sons, set off from Genoa on a voyage that would take him to the New World. Although Porto Vecchio (the old port area) had gradually fallen into disuse, an ambitious programme of regeneration in the late 1980s culminated in an International Exposition in 1992 that commemorated the 500th anniversary of Columbus's epoch-making voyage. Plans for Porto Vecchio's rejuvenation were drawn up by Renzo Piano, another famous son of Genoa, whose office is only a few hundred yards from the harbour. Significantly, and perhaps surprisingly, it was the first project he had undertaken in his native city.

Piano's strategy combines sensitive restoration and reuse with new elements designed in the robust maritime spirit of the existing port buildings, and thereby reconnecting the Porto Vecchio to the rest of the city. When operational, the port had been effectively isolated by an intrusive high-level motorway and surface road that cut a swathe along the harbour's eastern edge. The surface road was partially diverted into a tunnel, so that the ancient Piazza Caricamento, which mediates between port and city, was recolonized as a tranquil pedestrian square. The gorgeous trompe-l'oeil façade of the piazza's

Palazzo di San Giorgio, which housed one of the city's most powerful banks from 1408, was also restored as part of the recent regeneration.

Long piers have been characteristic of Genoa's harbour since ancient times, so Piano created a street that projects over the water. This modern version contains an aquarium and the Italian Pavilion, an exhibition and conference facility that resembles a huge ship docked in port. On the southern edge of the harbour, more conference and exhibition spaces were created in a quartet of seventeenth-century customs depositories (their painted elevations also handsomely restored) and a long warehouse that was originally used to store cotton.

The most visually arresting of the new structures is the Bigo. Rising dramatically from the water in front of the Piazza Caricamento, the Bigo is a colossal derrick composed of tapering steel booms that fan out in an expansive, exuberant gesture of welcome. The poised, angular members strung with tensile cables recall the forms of cranes and ships, reinforcing the nautical resonances. Two of the booms hold up the curving spars of a translucent tented roof, a carapace-like structure enclosing a short pier that functions as an events and performance space. The largest boom supports the cylindrical cab of a panoramic lift that offers fine views of the revitalized Porto Vecchio and the city beyond.

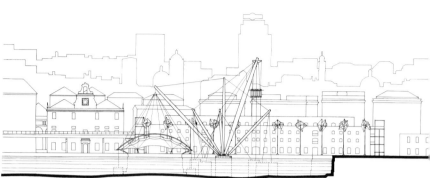

Sectional elevation

Left Combining elements of new construction with rehabilitation, conversion and archaeological revelation, Piano's scheme reconnects the old port with the life of the city and provides welcome open public spaces.

Above Sectional elevation of the harbour, showing the Bigo, tent and wind structures, with Palazzo di San Giorgio behind it.

Below The site plan illustrates the various components of the scheme.

1 The Bigo
2 Piazza del Feste (event space)
3 Piazza Caricamento
4 Palazzo di San Giorgio
5 Customs depositories
6 Cotton warehouse
7 Service spine
8 Navy building
9 Italian Pavilion
10 Aquarium

Site plan

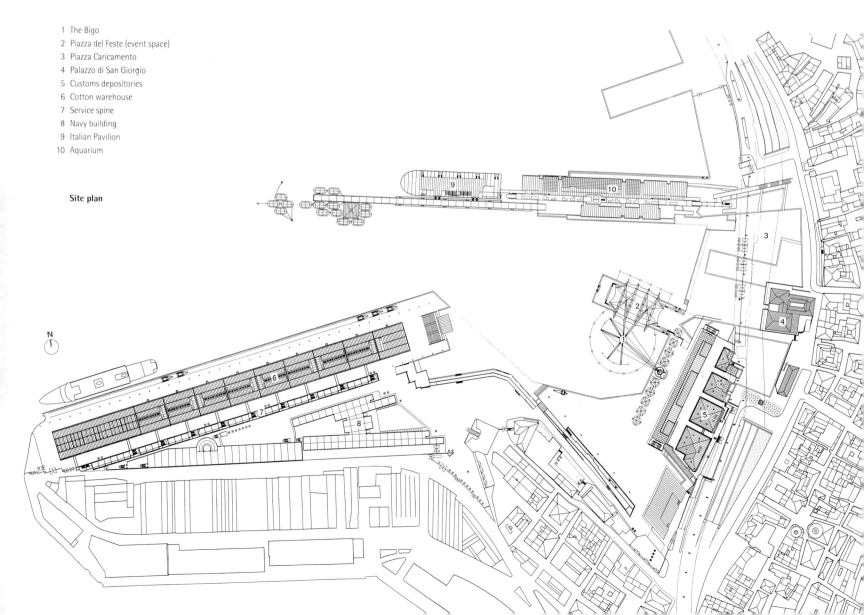

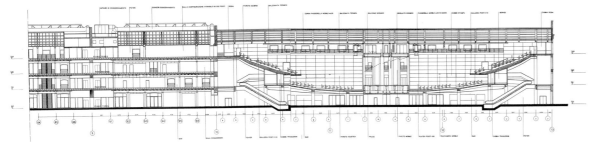

Cotton warehouse: long section

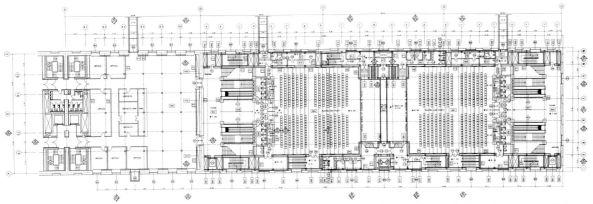

Cotton warehouse: auditorium-level plan (scale approx. 1:1000)

Above Part of the new service spine, which runs parallel with the refurbished cotton warehouse and is linked to it by a series of bridges. Crisp terra-cotta cladding alternates with glazing and louvres in a modern version of Genoa's tough port warehouse vernacular.

Left Plan and long section through the cotton warehouse which has been recolonized as a conference centre. The two large congress halls can be joined to make one vast auditorium.

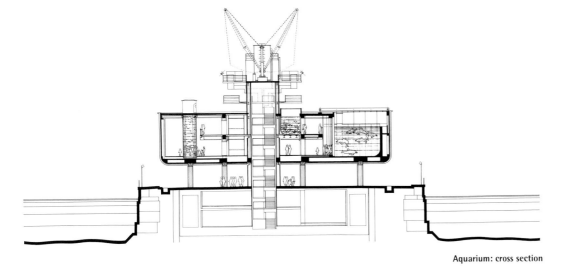

Aquarium: cross section

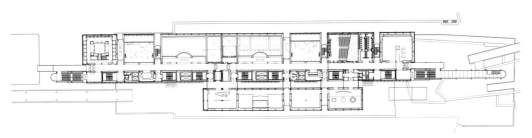

Aquarium: first-floor plan (scale approx. 1:2000)

Above Like a ship at berth, the aquarium juts out into the harbour.

Left Plan and cross section through the aquarium. The heavy water tanks are held aloft inside the raised, hull-like segments of its superstructure.

Century Tower

● Foster and Partners

● Tokyo, Japan

● 1991

Site plan

Top Bold and inscrutable, Century Tower rises serenely above Tokyo.

Above Site plan of the tower in its urban context.

Opposite Detail of the supple, curved roof that encloses the swimming pool and staff amenity section.

The Century Tower was Foster's first commission in Japan. The tower prompts comparisons with his epic Hongkong Bank – which in many ways was the symbolic genesis of the project – yet it also responds to very different cultural and urban factors.

Like a traditional Japanese haiku, Century Tower's seemingly simple form has an extreme, poetic intensity. Located in the northern Bunkyo-ku district of Tokyo, the building consists of two towers, nineteen and twenty-one storeys high, connected by an atrium – the architect calls it 'the slot' – crossed by a system of walkways. All floors are double height, a principle expressed in the structural strategy, which is based on a series of eccentrically braced frames, each two storeys high. These are articulated on the north and south elevations, as well as inside the atrium. Externally, the sculptural rhythm of the frames gives the tower its distinctive character, a modern abstraction of the large column halls and scaffold buildings of old Japan. Internally, the frames form a bridged portal between the service cores, leaving the floor space column-free and flexible. The frames also support mezzanine floors that are suspended within the two-storey structure.

Counterbalancing the structurally expressive main façades, the side elevations explore subtle variations of solid, void and transparency. The glazed west elevation contains a bank of lift shafts and transparent lift cars, whose constant movement animates the building's surface, like bubbles rising and falling. The east side is dedicated to functional elements, such as glazed escape stairs, louvred air-handling units and solid service riser shafts. On both side elevations the atrium registers as a transparent aperture precisely cleft into the tower's mass.

A soaring, nineteen-storey-high volume that diffuses light through the structure's heart, the atrium is the most daring and innovative element of Century Tower. Its exhilarating transparency, manipulation of light, subtle layering and depth of space embody the exquisitely refined spirit of Japanese interiors. The atrium also redefines spatial possibilities; prior to this design Japanese building restrictions dictated that an open shaft could not be combined with adjacent open floor space. But an innovative fire-engineering strategy of pressuring the atrium – to prevent smoke from entering in the event of a fire – along with the lift shafts and stairs, was used to overcome the existing legislation.

The tower's public lobby is double height and monochromatic, forming a generous light volume with stairs leading down to a small museum that houses the client's distinguished collection of Asian art. Beyond the lobby is a glazed roof, supported by an elegantly curving structure that encloses a swimming pool (part of the staff facilities) in the basement below. Foster's exploration of the potential of technology to orchestrate and enliven the working environment makes Century Tower a dynamic reappraisal of the speculative office block.

Right The swimming pool and staff amenities are enclosed in a separate block. The sensuous curve of the light-diffusing roof recalls traditional Japanese architecture.

Below The double-height volume of the entrance lobby cleft by the narrow slot of the towering atrium. On either side of the atrium are the eccentrically braced internal structural frames that enable the office space to be column-free. This type of frame is suitable for use in earthquake zones because, although it deforms, it does not collapse; however, the use of frames on such a scale was hitherto unprecedented and required rigorous engineering skill.

Opppositve, above The external articulation of the double-height structural frames resembles Japanese calligraphy in its reductivist intensity.

Opposite, below The plans and cross section reveal the penetrating slot of the atrium, and the mezzanine office levels slung from the structural frames. The column-free space generates an enviable flexibility that is further enhanced by confining services and circulation to the perimeter of the tower.

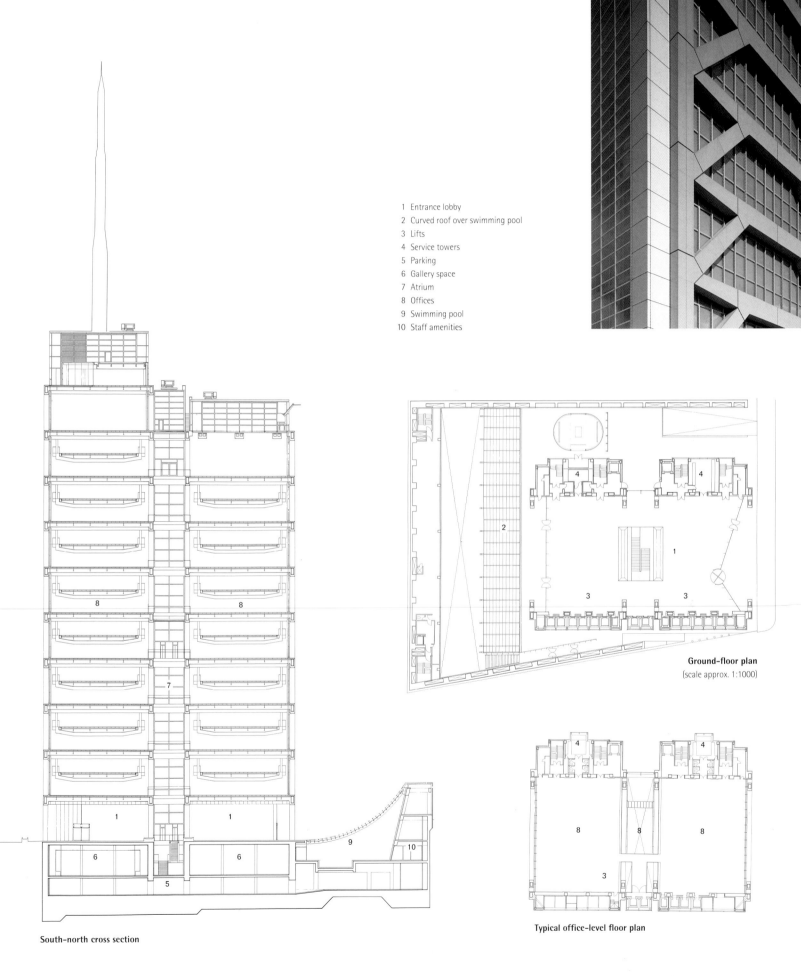

1 Entrance lobby
2 Curved roof over swimming pool
3 Lifts
4 Service towers
5 Parking
6 Gallery space
7 Atrium
8 Offices
9 Swimming pool
10 Staff amenities

Ground-floor plan
(scale approx. 1:1000)

Typical office-level floor plan

South-north cross section

Making Connections

The massive glazed vault at Waterloo
International Terminal, London, by Nicholas
Grimshaw and Partners (page 136)

Kansai Airport

Renzo Piano Building Workshop

Osaka, Japan

1994

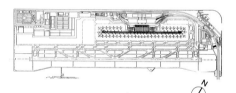

Site plan of artificial island

Top Traversed by a series of bridges, the impressively scaled canyon on the land side of the building links the various levels.

Middle Site plan of the artificial island in Osaka Bay built to accommodate the airport.

Above Poised lightly on its island, the building has the spare refinement of a glider.

Opposite One of the two great glazed gable walls. The simple yet elegant structure consists of bowstring trusses spanning vertically between the ground and the top chord of the sinuous roof truss.

Built to serve Japan's second most populous region, Kansai airport has been described as the first building of the twenty-first century, a claim given powerful legitimacy by the immense technical sophistication of its design and construction. Osaka's existing Itami airport reached full capacity years ago, but it was impossible to expand on the mainland, which is mountainous and densely populated. The solution's physical realization was an epic – almost biblical – feat of engineering: three mountains were demolished to provide the vast quantity of crushed rocks used to create the 511-hectare artificial island in Osaka Bay on which the new airport complex is located. The artificial island took five years to construct, and along with the Great Wall of China is one of only two man-made structures visible from space. The isolated location means that Kansai can operate twenty-four hours a day, the only airport in Japan able to do so, with consequent commercial benefits. Only one runway was built on the island, but it can handle 160,000 flights and twenty-five million passengers a year, making Kansai a major gateway to Japan and Southeast Asia.

Renzo Piano won the limited competition for the design of Kansai's terminal in 1988. From the air his extraordinary building appears as a symmetrical silver streak on the tabula rasa of the island. All the airport functions are accommodated in a single form: a sensuously undulating roof that resembles a breaking wave or a glider lightly poised for take-off. Its sleek organic form is a striking contrast to the complex, kit-of-parts nature of earlier Piano projects, such as the iconic Pompidou Centre (1977).

Kansai draws on Piano's research into building technologies that match the efficiency of nature, insights made possible by recent advances in mathematics and computing. This is most apparent in the building's distinctive geometry, which is derived from a pure toroidal form that made it possible to clad the entire curving roof surface in 82,000 stainless-steel panels of identical size. (The notion of self-similarity also has its origins in the natural world.)

The boarding wing's elongated sliver extends out from either side of a four-storey central terminal. From the land side, passengers are confronted by a soaring canyon that reveals the terminal's various levels and instils an immediate sense of organizational legibility. The space is extensively landscaped with trees, symbolizing an interaction between nature and technology. On the uppermost level, the billowing steel trusses enliven the vast international departures hall. Passengers work their way down through the terminal to the boarding wing at first-floor level, which has stunning views across the runway and spectacular internal vistas of the seemingly endless, fluid form.

An example of technology pushed to the limits, Kansai's graceful unity of space and structure embodies a breathtaking vision for the next millennium.

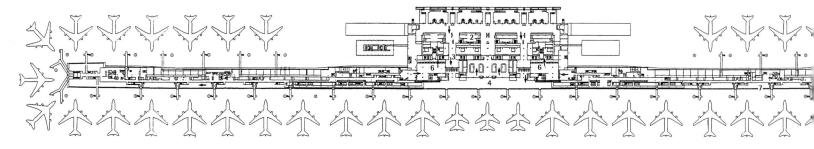

Plan of first-floor level: domestic arrivals and all boarding (scale approx. 1:8000)

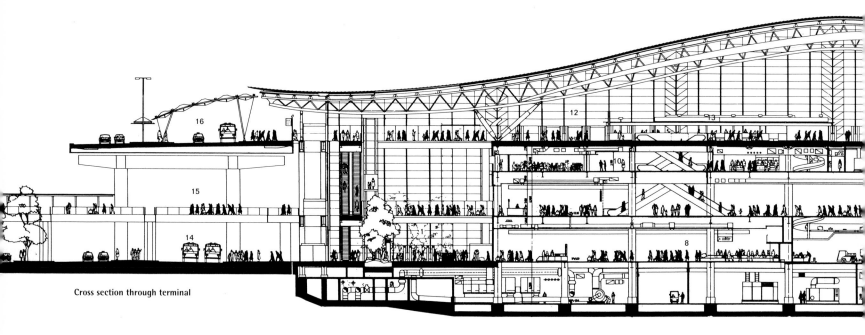

Cross section through terminal

1 Void of canyon
2 Domestic check-in counters
3 Domestic departures
4 Domestic boarding lounge
5 Domestic arrivals baggage collection
6 International arrivals immigration
7 International boarding lounge
8 International arrivals, baggage collection and customs
9 Domestic baggage handling
10 Non-duty-free shops and cafes
11 Duty-free shops
12 International departures hall
13 Check-in counters
14 Arrivals collection
15 Bridge from station
16 Departures drop-off

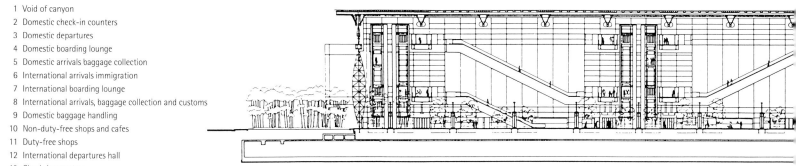

Long section through terminal (canyon)

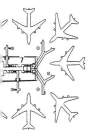

Right The air-side wall of the terminal, with the stainless-steel tiles of the roof projecting out to shade the curving glass skin.

Left Plan of first-floor level showing the relationship of the main terminal building to the elongated boarding wing.

Below Cross section through the terminal illustrates the generous sweep of the roof. The huge trusses are supported by clusters of splayed props. The land-side canyon acts as the main organizational device, filtering and directing passengers to the appropriate level.

Bottom Long section through the imposing canyon with its dramatic array of lifts and escalators.

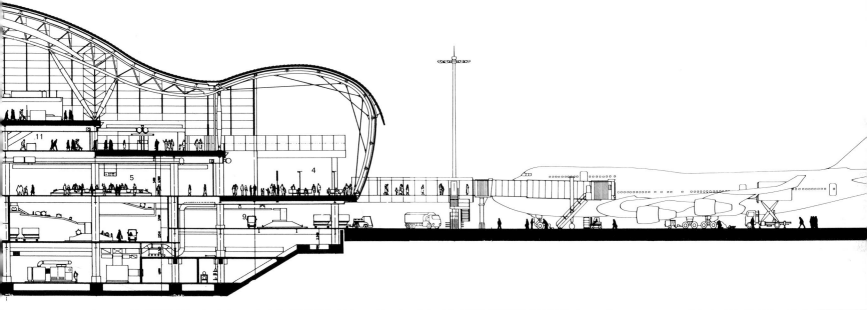

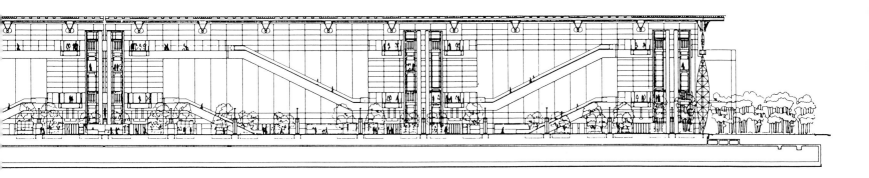

Above The billowing, light-filled terminal interior. Conceived as a soft machine, the building was shaped by its function, a design made possible by advances in computers and mathematics. The asymmetrical curve of the arched trusses follows the decelerating curve of the jets of fresh air that ventilate the huge space and control its background temperature. The air is captured by scoop-like fabric shells suspended from the trusses. These also act as reflectors for the uplighters that illuminate the space. Structure, space, services and skin are conjoined in an indissoluble unity.

Right The seemingly infinite vista of the 1.7-kilometre-long boarding wing, possibly the longest single volume ever built. The curves in both cross and long section, together with a structure pushed to new limits of lightness achieve a grace and loftiness equal to that of the great Gothic cathedrals.

Waterloo Station International Terminal

- Nicholas Grimshaw and Partners
- London, England
- 1993

Top Detail of the station canopy. Rectangular sheets of glass, overlapping at the top and bottom like roof tiles, are joined at their sides by concertina-shaped neoprene gaskets that can flex and expand to accommodate the curved configuration.

Above Grimshaw's early sketch explores the organic, asymmetric properties of the station vault.

Opposite Although a clear descendant of the Victorian train shed, Waterloo's tapering span and narrow, sinuous plan are an ingeniously engineered response to the site and track layout. The complexity of the roof structure, which curves in two directions, necessitated 229 different sizes of glass sheets out of a total of 1680 used – yet much more would have been required if a tight carapace had been adopted instead of a loose-fitting skin.

Following page The glazed maw of the vault at dusk resembles a glowing, animate creature burrowing into the existing station. Amid the bleary dislocation of Waterloo, the terminal appears as a striking new city landmark.

The International Terminal at Waterloo was designed to receive rail traffic from Europe through the Channel Tunnel link. Conceptually and architecturally the terminal is a singular achievement, particularly because the British economic and political climate has been hostile to rail transport for over fifteen years. From the first outline proposals to the fixing of the last piece of glass, the building's creation has been an act of sustained cooperative imagination and daring that recalls the great engineering structures of the nineteenth century.

Although Nicholas Grimshaw's curvaceous, delicately faceted train shed clearly has its origins in the cavernous Victorian iron-and-glass train-station vaults, in terms of planning and people-handling Waterloo International has more in common with an airport: the terminal can accommodate up to fifteen million passengers a year, at a peak of six thousand an hour – more, for example, than Heathrow's Terminal Four – and the brief stipulated that the departure time (including the passport, customs and baggage checks) should be no more than twenty minutes.

Large sections of Waterloo's warren of Victorian brick vaulting were demolished to make way for the new four-level structure. To cope with the dynamic stresses of the 400-metre long Eurostar trains passing in and out of the station a huge concrete viaduct was created, forming the plinth for the train shed and providing the volume to contain the segregated arrivals and departures levels. Early concept designs placed the departures level above

the railway tracks, but these were later superseded by locating the passenger halls underneath the glass vault.

After checking in, passengers emerge from the subterranean, airport-style lounges into the exhilarating luminosity of the station vault. Remarkably, it accounted for only ten per cent of the overall budget. Seen from the air, the great glazed funnel appears to gnaw its way into the existing roofscape of Waterloo Station, like a giant caterpillar greedily devouring a leaf. More prosaically, it is an exceptionally sophisticated piece of engineering, elegantly accommodating five eccentrically curving railway tracks and a variable span.

The vault's basic structure is essentially a flattened, three-pin arch that consists of two bowstring trusses. Because of the asymmetrical geometry of the platforms, the centre pin is moved to one side, allowing the arch to rise steeply on the west side to provide height clearance for the trains, while inclining gently over the platforms on the east side. The curved carapace is clad in a combination of glass panels and stainless-steel decking, a loose-fitting skin specially designed by computers to adapt to the twisting nature of the structure.

Although curving train sheds are not in themselves remarkable (John Dobson and Robert Stephenson's Newcastle Central Station spanned 60 metres on a curve as early as 1850), Waterloo International's innovative resolution of a set of complex conditions represents new heights of engineering skill and architectural vision.

Below At its widest point the vault spans 48.5 metres, reducing to 32.7 metres as the tracks narrow. Thirty-six sets of bowstring arches make up the vault structure, which had to be capable of sustaining the collapse of an arch in the event of an accident. Each arch is formed from two bowstring trusses, one effectively turned 'inside out' to accommodate the curved plan and to provide clearance over the trains on the outer tracks.

Right Cross section through the terminal shows the relationship of the train shed to the passenger halls and ticketing area below. An original proposal inverted this arrangement, so that the trains were underground. The section also reveals the configuration of the three-pinned bowstring arches.

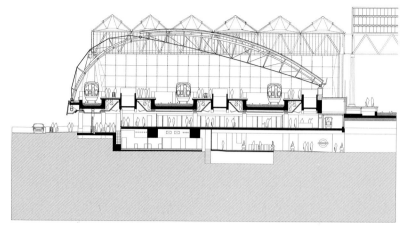

Cross section

1 Ticket hall
2 Lower concourse
3 Ticket check
4 Security check
5 Departure hall
6 Arrivals/departures central area
7 Ramp from arrivals hall to new concourse
8 Escalator link with Waterloo
9 Lifts
10 Station vault
11 Glazed end wall

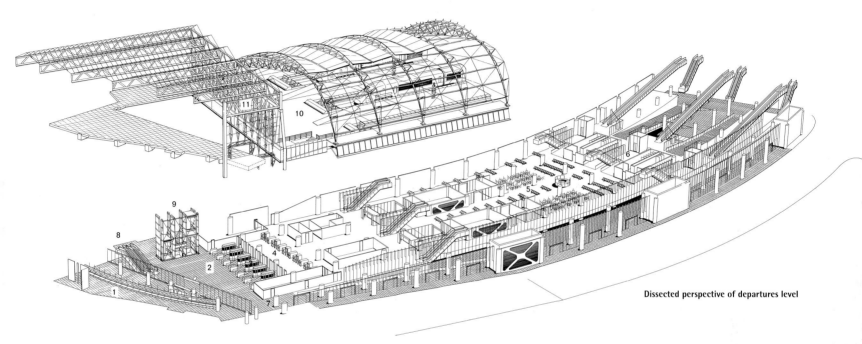

Dissected perspective of departures level

Above Dissected perspective of the departures level and part of the station vault. The sequence of passenger processing is based on the airport model of security checks, departure lounges and boarding at specified gates. Banks of escalators and lifts take passengers up to platform level, where they have a brief opportunity to savour the airy vault of the station canopy before their train departs. Arriving passengers follow the same sequence in reverse, being funnelled down to the arrivals level below the departure area, which connects with road, rail and underground links.

Right Detail of the glazed end wall between the existing Waterloo concourse and the new terminal, which permits spectacular views down the length of the train shed. The corner of the wall is supported on a new steel A frame (see perspective above). The structure of the wall is surprisingly delicate: stainless-steel bowstring trusses take the vertical and horizontal loads of the glass down to the steel base and up to a new horizontal wind girder on the edge of the old roof.

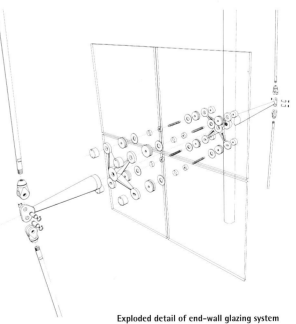

Exploded detail of end-wall glazing system

Marseilles Airport

- Richard Rogers Partnership
- Marseilles, France
- 1992

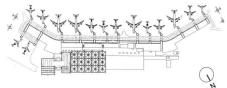

Overall plan

Top The building takes it cues from the pragmatism of engineering rather than any formal architectural tradition.

Above Overall plan of the airport shows the eastern extension, at top left, and the umbrella-like roof structure of the proposed *coeur*.

Opposite, above left Plan of departure level and cross section through departure lounges. The arrivals route runs at upper level through the double-height volume of the departure lounge, preserving security segregation but allowing the two groups of passengers to share and enjoy the same space.

Opposite, above right The departure lounge and the elevated arrivals walkway. The roof is supported by a series of lightweight steel bowstring trusses.

Opposite, below Airplanes dock into glazed boarding piers that are crowned by top-lit drums.

Like most airports, Marseilles' has evolved in an unsatisfactory piecemeal fashion. The clean lines of the original 1950s terminal building have long since been overwhelmed by a succession of undistinguished extensions built to cope with rapidly increasing traffic (Marseilles is the largest airport in France outside Paris). In 1988 local architects Atelier 9 and ETA drew up a masterplan, the so-called *coeur*, which was essentially a large shopping mall that would attract the regular flow of passengers. The Richard Rogers Partnership was initially called in to give the *coeur* a spectacular architectural identity, but instead the practice effectively rewrote the brief and embarked on devising an alternative expansion strategy for the entire airport. Based on a linear plan that links and unifies the existing terminal buildings by an air-side walkway, their proposal included two new buildings at each end. The first of these, an extension to the domestic terminal at the eastern end of the airport, has been completed in partnership with Atelier 9 and ETA.

Through pragmatic planning and imaginative handling of space and materials, Rogers has managed to transcend the architectural inhibitions of airport security. The absolute requirement for the arriving and departing passengers to be physically segregated is met by channelling them on to different levels – departures on the first floor, arrivals on the second and baggage claim on the ground level – but allowing them to share the same expansive double-height space, a great transparent cavern filled with activity. This simple tactic of vertical circulation has also been used recently by Rogers at the Europier terminal at London's Heathrow airport (1995).

The building's expression of structure and services are legible internally and externally. The roof over the lounge is supported by exposed bowstring steel trusses engineered by Peter Rice of Ove Arup & Partners; the tautly curving trusses rest on round steel columns. On the building's east side there is no enclosed walkway to provide intermediate support. Instead, slimmer, vertical versions of the bowstring trusses are used to stiffen the mullions of the external wall, articulating a unified structural language. The building's narrow and high proportions permit daylight to penetrate its centre without the need for roof lights, so the entire roof area is available for services routing. The ductwork and air-handling plant are mounted on top of a sub-grid of steel beams, giving the terminal an expressive nuts-and-bolts quality that recalls Fleetguard, PA Technology and other quasi-industrial sheds of the 1980s. Yet here the more refined articulation of the components generates a softer, subtler, more organic composition despite its apparent functionalism.

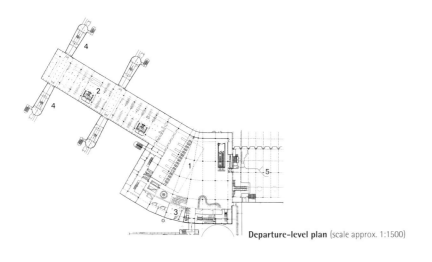

Departure-level plan (scale approx. 1:1500)

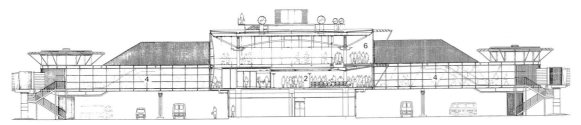

Cross section

1 Security check
2 Departure lounges
3 Cafe
4 Boarding piers
5 Existing airport building
6 Arrivals level

Lyons Airport TGV Station

Santiago Calatrava

Lyons, France

1995

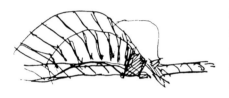

Top The biomorphic concrete subterranean platform vault. To achieve a seamless finish and minimize the number of joints, the structure was cast in situ, using twenty-five different sets of steel shuttering. Basic prototypes of each element were originally cast in timber shuttering, working to Calatrava's preliminary drawings. These were shaped and modified by hand, and then mathematical coordinates taken from the finalized prototypes were used to produce a computer-generated three-dimensional form for each segment.

Above Calatrava's evocative preliminary sketch of the bird-like form of the station hall.

Opposite The exhilarating interior of the station hall with its curving, dihedral roof. Light is diffused through the massive glazed end walls and a series of triangular incisions in the roof.

Compared with the dismaying British experience of an ailing and increasingly fragmented rail system, French railways are a model of state-backed progressiveness. The country's commitment to developing its national network of high-speed links and stations is epitomized by the TGV station at Lyons's Satolas airport in the central Rhône-Alpes region. Located on a new section of track that filters high-speed trains off the Paris-Lyons main line to Valence, further south, the airport and its station are seen as an important national gateway. Commensurate with this increase in status was the commissioning of Santiago Calatrava design the station. He responded with a typically ebullient, gestural building that attempts to instill the potentially demoralizing experience of modern travel with a sense of dignity and excitement.

The station's guts are buried in a cut of land just east of the airport's main runway and terminal buildings. The interchange is largely underground, to allow for future runway extensions over the main railway. Tracks and platforms are enclosed by a shallow 500-metre-long concrete-rib lattice resembling a surprisingly delicate skeleton. The 50-metre-wide platform vault is surmounted by the dihedral wings of the monumental station hall, like a giant bird of prey, marking the gateway to the complex. The great wings radiate from a central spine, forming a pair of skewed cantilevering roofs

articulated by a filigree of steel support members. The side walls are glazed, suffusing the interior with light.

Romantically analogous to the act of flying, the station hall recalls the swooping, biomorphic fluidity of Eero Saarinen's iconic TWA terminal (1956–62) at New York's John F. Kennedy airport. Compared with Saarinen's structure, though, Calatrava's is an altogether more angular, almost robotic creation. The use of steel, with its intrinsic rigidity, rather than the concrete of the exquisitely organic platform vault, must account for the apparent stiltedness. The sensation of standing on the platforms is rather like being inside the bleached ribcage of a prehistoric behemoth.

The sinuous lattice vault structure is punctuated by diamond-shaped apertures designed to channel as much natural light as possible into the interior. To minimize the number of joints and achieve a seamless finish, the vault was largely cast in situ, rather than assembled from precast elements. Twenty-five different sets of steel shutters were conceived to match the intricacies of the design.

Despite its size, the building is essentially a magnification of Calatrava's elemental roof and pavilion forms adopted in a modern hybrid – a traditional train-station vault recast as a monument to the ever-seductive power of air travel.

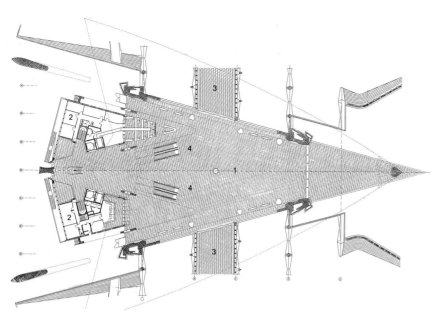

Concourse-level floor plan (scale approx. 1:1000)

1 Main concourse
2 Offices
3 Concourse to platforms below
4 Escalators to upper level

Opposite, above The floor plan shows how the station hall is a transit space from where passengers proceed down to the platforms.

Opposite, below Perched like a predatory bird on the platform vault, the striking, gestural form of the new station emphasizes Lyons's renewed civic and economic importance.

Right Site plan illustrating the station in relation to the airport. The two are linked by an enclosed elevated walkway.

Below A section through the long platform vault reveals the rhythmic, organic complexity of the structure.

Bottom Long section through the station hall. The elevated walkway link to the airport is reached by escalators from the station concourse. At platform level the outside tracks are used by airport trains and the central tracks (enclosed by a box tunnel) by nonstopping TGV services that pass through the station at 300 kilometres/hour.

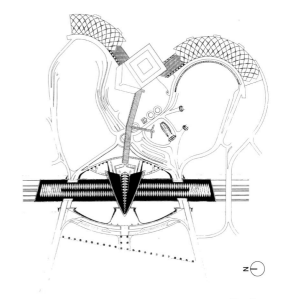

Site plan

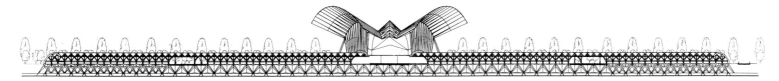

Combined long section through the platform vault and cross section through the station hall

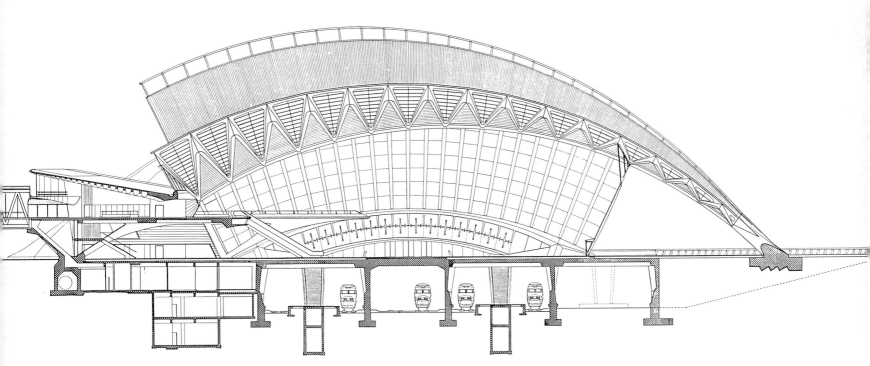

Long section through the station hall

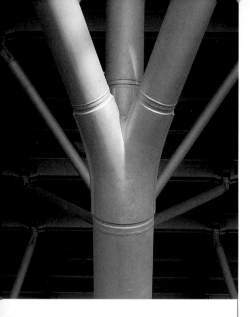

Stuttgart Airport

- Von Gerkan Marg and Partners
- Stuttgart, Germany
- 1991

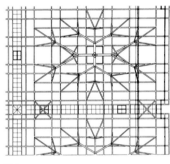

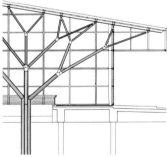

Plan and section of typical structural bay

Top Detail of one of the branch-like supports that form part of the structural 'trees'.

Above Plan and section of a typical structural bay. Nine bays enclose the main arrivals and departures hall.

Opposite The arboreal structure orders and enlivens the bustling volume of the main hall.

Airport design can be seen as an extension of landscape architecture. By definition airports are highly visible from both the ground and the air, and so have the potential to be experienced more broadly than most types of building. Stuttgart airport has drawn on this metaphor to create a highly poetic, artificial landscape that humanizes and dramatizes the act of flying.

From the air, the terminal resembles a huge sloping wing or hillock in the flat fields outside Stuttgart. The building mass is divided into two volumes – a large hall, trapezoidal in section, that houses the basic arrivals and departures procedures, and a low-lying, linear sequence of lounges from which travellers are bussed to waiting aircraft. The main hall gently rises up at an angle to overlap with the smaller linear volume, while internally their zone of intersection is marked by a series of semicircular terraces – containing shops, restaurants, conference rooms, VIP lounges and other incidental facilities – that bulge out into the main hall. The squat linear volume is clad in stone, forming a solid, almost rusticated base of the lighter, more ethereal central concourse.

The Stuttgart airport was completed within weeks of Norman Foster's Stansted (page 158), and the two buildings display similar formal and organizational preoccupations. For instance, both structures are designed to be seen as object buildings in the landscape.

Also, the main circulation routes through both terminals were conceived as direct, linear paths from land to air side. The most obvious similarity, however, is Von Gerkan Marg's adoption of a tree-like structural system that supports the giant sloping roof of the main concourse and opens up the spatial and structural possibilities of a services-free roof space, as at Stansted. Here, the roof is divided into twelve rectangular bays, each of which is supported by a set of splayed-steel members converging in sturdy vertical trunks. Von Gerkan Marg's structures are more overtly arboreal, displaying both a greater structural complexity and a more clearly emphasized hierarchy of members, from twigs to branches to trunks. The angular trees transform the bustling concourse into a futuristic forest, accentuated by the elaborate networks arrestingly silhouetted against the terminal's glazed walls.

The south elevation, overlooking the runway, is screened by broad strips of aerofoil-shaped louvres that can be automatically adjusted to control incoming daylight. The louvres also help to articulate the bold south elevation, refining the rusticated base of the linear departures building. Stuttgart is a modest regional airport, so all its functions were condensed within a single terminal; by contrast, Stansted is planned around a shuttle-linked complex of satellite buildings. Yet both are invigorating interpretations of the airport typology.

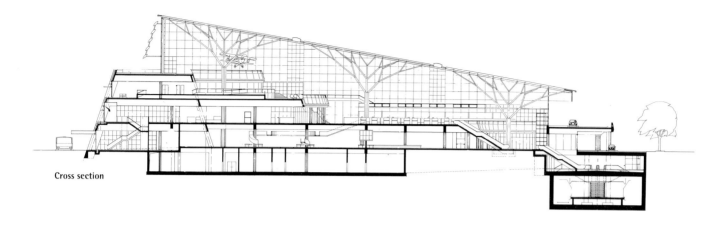

Cross section

Opposite, above Cross section through the arrivals and departures hall. The stepped arrangement of spaces follows the line of the sloping roof. The form of the tree-like structural bays was developed by computer modelling. The angles of the branches reflects the line of force as the weight of the roof is transmitted to the foundations.

Opposite, below The carefully ordered hierarchy of the air side with its deeply recessed windows and regimented lines of *brises soleils*. The lighter volume of the main hall rises above the squat, rusticated base of the boarding wing.

Right The building's wedge-shaped profile gives it a measure of presence in the flat landscape. The wedge also acts as an acoustic barrier.

Below Plan of the departures hall. The compact plan makes circulation simple and legible. A linear route leads through check-in and security processing and then on to the boarding wing and departure lounges.

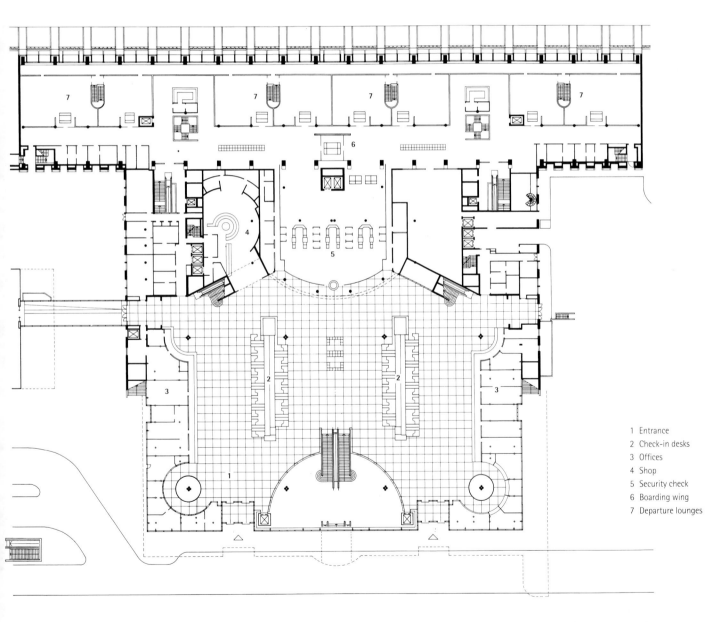

1 Entrance
2 Check-in desks
3 Offices
4 Shop
5 Security check
6 Boarding wing
7 Departure lounges

Departure-level floor plan (scale approx. 1:1000)

Ferry Terminal

- Will Alsop and me di um Architects
- Hamburg, Germany
- 1993

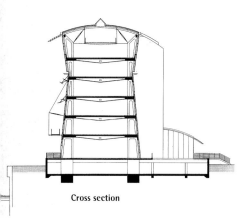

Cross section

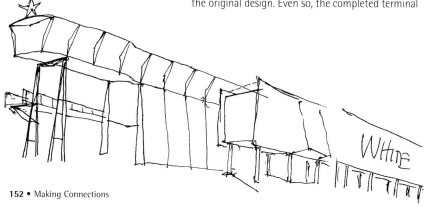

Hamburg has always been one of Germany's most important maritime trading cities, yet like all ports it has had to respond to immense changes. During the 1970s heavy shipping moved farther down the Elbe, leaving the seaport derelict, but the area has gradually been regenerated and gentrified by a mixture of housing, service-sector industries and tourist attractions. In the late 1980s a competition was held for a shipping terminal on a stretch of quayside along the Elbe to house facilities for Hamburg's small ferry fleet and a North Sea cruise ship company. Alsop's initial, winning proposal was a powerful response to the seaside site's romance and function, which were reinforced by his own experience of dock and harbour projects. Memories of mists, tempests and voyages were literally transcribed into the rounded profile of a distinctly nautical structure.

The programme and the site made it possible to think big and, above all, differently, but subsequent programme changes and cost reductions had the effect of simplifying the original design. Even so, the completed terminal

(developed with the Hamburg firm me di um) still makes a bracing impact. Extending longitudinally along the quayside, the building exudes a confident air, its horizontal orientation inspired by the ferries and cruise liners that dock alongside it. The double-height ground floor is completely glazed, allowing an unimpeded view from the waiting areas to the water and ships beyond.

The site's damp, salty air mitigated against the use of a steel frame, so the structure is made from reinforced concrete. Prefabricated in Germany and Denmark, a series of massive concrete porticoes divide the 200-metre-long building into thirty-two sections. Each portico is formed by two A-frame column arrangements joined together by shallow, inverted V-shaped trusses on which the floor slabs rest. The tapering concrete A-frame structure is partially revealed on the riverside elevation and at the terminal's eastern end, where the columns slant expressively to support the projecting volume of the second- and third-floor offices above.

Travellers board the ferries via a translucent tube that snakes towards the dock from the building's western end. The unified effect of all these elements – the external staircase, A-frame supports, metal ramps, balconies and *brises soleils* – is a seamless blending into the surrounding portscape, and yet Alsop's terminal invigorates the area with its bold massing, welcoming transparency and a tectonic muscularity that pays tribute to Hamburg's maritime past and present.

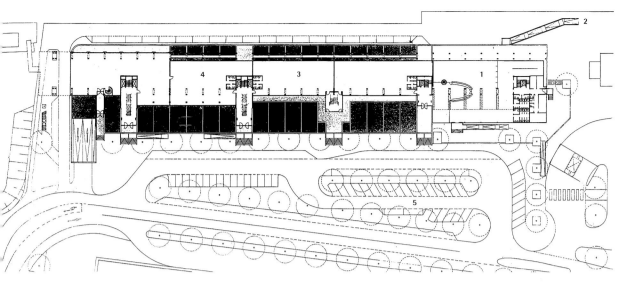

Left The 200 metre-long building extends along the quayside and can be subdivided easily across its structural bays

Ground-floor plan (scale approx. 1:1500)

1 Ferry terminal
2 Passenger access to ships
3 Cruise ship terminal
4 Cruise ship centre
5 Car park

Above The concrete frame is infilled with aluminium panels and green-tinted glazing. Adjustable sun louvres are attached to the south-facing, dock-side elevation.

Left Supported by the A-frame concrete structure, an elevated walkway runs along the dock-side elevation, adding to the maritime overtones.

Opposite, above The terminal's form mixes nautical resonances with the vernacular solidity of Hamburg's port warehouses.

Opposite, middle The cross section shows the configuration of the structural porticoes. A-frame columns are joined to shallow, inverted trusses.

Opposite, bottom Alsop's original sketch of the terminal.

Euralille Station

- SNCF Architects
- Lille, France
- 1994

Above The curved station roof is straddled by a bizarrely boot-shaped office block designed by Christian Portzamparc, just one element in Rem Koolhaas's visionary masterplan for Euralille. The presence of the new, high-speed train line, coupled with Lille's fortunate geography, propels the city into the new role of major European transport node.

Opposite, above The cross section highlights the relationship of the subterranean platforms to the concourse and roof. Through trains are enclosed in a central tunnel.

Opposite, below Escalators link the concourse with the platform levels below. The sides of the central, through-train tunnel (on the left) are perforated by elongated arches. The paired arches of the intricate, wave-like roof structure punctuate the cavernous space.

The routing of the high-speed (TGV) train line from Paris through northern France to connect with the Channel Tunnel incited French mayors to haggle over its progress through their cities. Ultimately, Lille won the honour, and with it the prospect of elevating a city of decaying heavy industry to a major European transport node. This set in motion an ambitious urban make-over of part of the city centre, masterminded by Rem Koolhaas. The Dutch architect's Euralille (a name that exudes appropriate overtones of European homogeneity) is a fetishistically monumental agglomeration of offices, shops, housing and entertainment facilities arranged on what was once a vacant swathe of land near the existing nineteenth-century Lille-Flanders station. The pivotal element of Koolhaas's scheme, however, is Lille-Europe, a major new TGV station capable of handling fifteen thousand passengers a day.

Drawing on the archetypal station form, the long structure is enveloped by a sinuously curving glass roof that extends 270 metres along the railway tracks and is interrupted at right angles by three huge and rather self-conscious towers, landmarks for Euralille. Above the tracks is an arcade-like precinct, connected at intervals by escalators to the station platforms below. The elevated concourse opens like a balcony towards the eastern side of Lille, offering views of the old city skyline. Beneath the concourse is a Piranesian world of stairs, ramps and escalators, connecting the station with buses, taxis, car parking and the Lille metro.

Hovering diaphanously above the concourse, the roof is infused with light from the changing skies of northern France, transforming the building into something resembling a living organism. A filigree of cables is attached to extraordinarily slender tubular-steel arches, giving the effect of what the station's architect, Jean-Marie Duthilleul, conceived as 'fine lace floating above the train'. His lyrical notion has been splendidly realized by Peter Rice working with Ove Arup & Partners.

The distinctive wave-profile roof consists of paired steel arches set at 12-metre centres that bear on the podium's concrete structure. Cross-bracing ties provide longitudinal stability and prevent the arches from buckling. To sustain the illusion of the floating roof, the arches are connected to longitudinal roof beams with cable ties rather than struts. Thin strips of glass cladding, separated by steel troughs formed into the double curves, serve to emphasize the structure's transparent, immaterial quality. Radiant, particularly at night, the roof captures the hectic activities of Lille's newest *quartier* below. Like a traditional quayside, the concourse effectively combines the bustle of the city with the lingering romance of train travel.

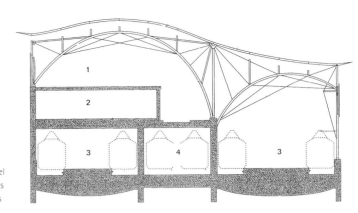

1 Entrance level
2 Concourse level
3 Stopping trains
4 Through trains

Cross section

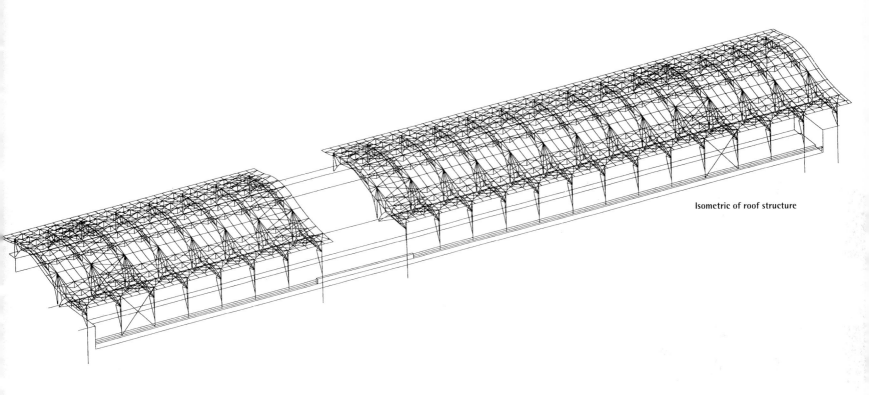

Isometric of roof structure

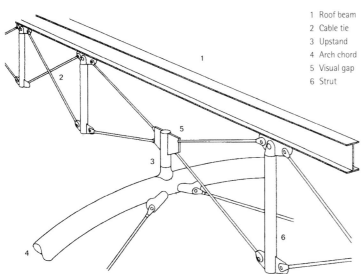

1 Roof beam
2 Cable tie
3 Upstand
4 Arch chord
5 Visual gap
6 Strut

Detail of arch-to-roof beam connection

Opposite Detail of the vast, luminous roof. Its sense of insubstantiality is achieved with the use of thin glass strips that are separated and supported by steel troughs formed into double curves. The troughs bear on the longitudinal beams and are covered externally with expanded metal and internally with perforated aluminium panels. This gives a smooth finish in which the curves are emphasized by the delicate pattern of the perforations.

Left Detail of arch-to-roof beam connection. As the roof is intended to float over the station, connections to the longitudinal roof beams are made with cable ties as opposed to struts. The arches do not actually touch the beams; hence the sensation of a hovering roof. The roof beams are also stiffened by ties attached to short, descending struts.

Above Isometric projection of the roof structure. The structure is based on paired steel arches set at 12 metres centres. The slender tubular arches bear on the concrete lower structure and to props in the glazed west wall. They are prevented from buckling by ties and cross bracing that gives the entire structure longitudinal stability.

Stansted Airport

- Foster and Partners
- Stansted, England
- 1991

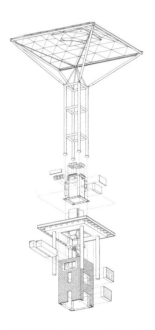

Top Detail of the roof structure. The crucial connecting component is the so-called 'Jesus nut' at the apex of the structure that rigidly braces the members in the correct position.

Above Exploded axonometric of a structural tree shows the relationship between structure and services.

Opposite The act of arrival is celebrated. A row of structural trees extends beyond the building to support a porte-cochère that serves as a triumphal archway to passengers arriving at the main concourse level.

Stansted is London's third airport, tucked away in the flat Essex countryside, a forty-minute train ride from central London's Liverpool Street station. Unlike the bewildering, loutish agglomerations of Heathrow and Gatwick, Stansted is compact, singular and civilized, a meticulously calculated homage to the enduring thrill of air travel. It was clear that Norman Foster's love of flying and penchant for bold ideas made him the perfect candidate to design Stansted, a mammoth task that included re-evaluating the airport's organizational principles.

The outcome is a central building linked to a series of satellite terminals by an automated rail shuttle. As Stansted expands, new terminals will be added; the central building can itself be extended lengthways by adding on structural bays. This ordered, logical approach aims to minimize the effects of piecemeal development that afflict so many modern airports.

Stansted's simplicity is its genius, a poetic restatement of Foster's ability to distil fundamental elements from enormously complex programmes. The architectural and organizational solutions appear natural and self-evident, inspired to some extent by a romantic view of the earliest days of flying, when passengers simply strode across the runway to their waiting plane from a Nissen hut.

Public facilities are arranged on a single concourse floor with arrivals and departures planned side by side. This has numerous advantages: it generates a compact building form, greatly reduces walking distances, assists orientation and allows passengers to move easily through the terminal on linear routes. Below the main concourse is a complex undercroft housing baggage-handling, service areas, an environmental engineering plant and commercial storage. In an elegant resolution of utilities and structure, service pods are integrated within the square trunks and fed from the basement plant.

Because the services are placed underground, the roof space is free to become the dominant visual element, with breathtaking results. A grid of shallow domes gently undulates above the concourse like a billowing tent. Roof lights in the lattice structure of each dome module diffuse natural light into the halls below, animating the bustling public spaces with an exquisite translucency. The domes are supported by square clusters of white tubular-steel columns on a 36-metre-square grid, while the tops of the columns spread out diagonally to meet the domes, their angular spars delicately tapering at the ends. Repeated throughout the terminal, the columns resemble sheltering trees or outstretched hands.

On the north side of the terminal a row of structural trees extends beyond the glass wall to form a dramatic porte-cochère, instilling a sense of arrival and sheltering passengers. Foster has succeeded in translating the sheer excitement of taking to the air into sophisticated reality, and this exuberance, together with an impressive formal and organizational rigour, makes Stansted an exceptional achievement: British airports have come of age.

1 Railway station
2 Porte-cochère
3 Main concourse
4 Ticket desks
5 Security check
6 Departure lounge
7 Shuttle to satellites
8 Air-side operations offices
9 Baggage handling
10 General storage
11 Plant
12 Loading bay
13 To car park and bus station

Below North-south cross section. Underpinning the organization of the terminal was the desire to avoid the disorientation typical of most modern airports. Foster's design evokes the simplicity and convenience of the early days of flying. All public areas are on a single-level concourse, so progress through the building is a direct linear route from one side to the other. Baggage handling, plant and storage are located in the undercroft. Services are conveyed up into the concourse through the structural trees, an elegant and inventive handling of the scale and diversity of services required in such a large public space. The centre of the trees contains a service stair, providing easy access for maintenance.

Bottom The elegant, Miesian pavilion in the landscape articulated by the imposing structural trees. Foster originally proposed an entirely transparent building, but as executed only the arrivals (south) and air-side (north) elevations are fully transparent. The east and west sides have clear glazing at lower levels, with milky translucent panels above to achieve the necessary solar shading. This has served to strengthen the directional pull from the entrance to the air side.

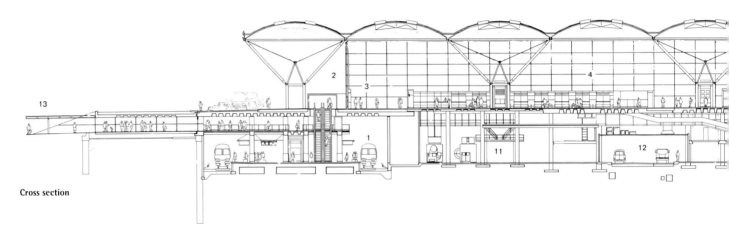

Cross section

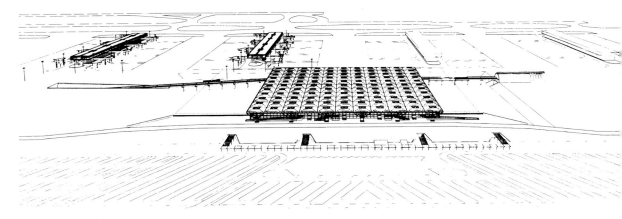

Aerial perspective of site

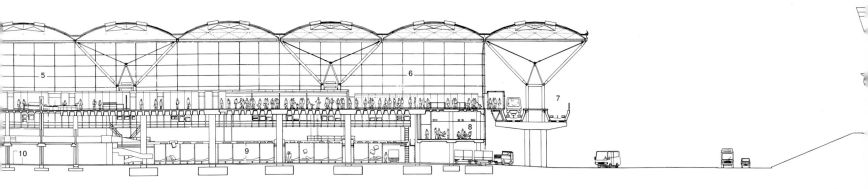

Top Aerial perspective of the overall airport site, including the main terminal and the satellites. The satellites are linked to the terminal by a shuttle rail system. This arrangement overcomes the problem of piecemeal expansion – as Stansted grows, new satellites are built as needed. The terminal can also be extended longitudinally, by adding on structural bays.

Right The roofscape billows gently like a tent over the concourse. Each 18-metre-square roof shell includes four triangular apertures that flood the concourse with reflected natural light. During the day, this provides enough illumination for most purposes, with consequent energy-saving advantages. Uplighters on the structural trees provide supplementary lighting as required. The result is a great glass shed that is full of an elusive, shifting, magical play of light.

Civic Symbolism

Richard Rogers's European Court of Human
Rights in Strasbourg (page 178)

Regional Government Centre

William Alsop Architects

Marseilles, France

1994

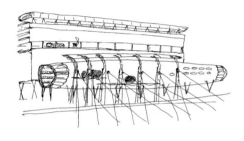

Top Alsop's radically subjective approach to form-making is inspired by his paintings and sketches rather than analyses of data. Shapes are made to work structurally, as opposed to being the logical expression of an engineering solution. Technology is appropriated as required to create particular effects, giving his buildings a curiously scenographic quality.

Above The form of the building is gradually becoming apparent in this early sketch.

Opposite The chasm between the *Administratif* office block and the *Délibératif* debating chamber, the elements that make up the complex. Tubular bridges connect the two parts. The triangular, colour-coated steel cladding on the *Déliberatif* has an extraordinary iridescence, like fish scales. The intensity of the blue exterior is like a distillation of the Mediterranean sky.

Renowned as a brilliant maverick but with few built projects to his name, London-based architect Will Alsop broke into the big league with this major French commission. His competition-winning scheme for a government centre in Marseilles combines civic grandeur with political symbolism in a bravura interplay of form and technology. Although Alsop cannot be described as a card-carrying High-Tech adherent, he makes technology work in the service of imagination, a radically subjective approach that begins with the free association of painting to suggest potential building forms. Extreme abstractions are distilled into built reality, a process that might seem starkly at odds with a demanding and politically sensitive programme. Despite the (possibly inevitable) fact that the completed project is not as explosively eccentric as his original design, Alsop's building still oozes originality and a perverse, heroic quirkiness amid the amorphous suburbs of Marseilles.

The complex consists of a cigar-shaped assembly hall (the *Délibératif*), mounted on pairs of splayed legs, and two more conventionally formed office blocks that contain administrative functions (the *Administratif*). Surmounting the larger of the two office blocks is another curiously organic structure – like a squashed Swiss roll – that houses the local politicians' offices and the council president's apartment. All the component parts are clad in searing cobalt blue panels, giving the building a shocking, painterly intensity.

The panels cladding one side of the *Délibératif* are triangular, like shimmering fish scales, an effect that reinforces the building's zoomorphism. On the other side, the skin has been peeled away to reveal the *Délibératif*'s deformed ovoid structure; stretched over this ribcage are white fabric awnings designed to protect the debating chamber from heat gain. The two blocks of the *Administratif* enclose a generously proportioned atrium, in which the building's colour scheme changes from the exterior's vibrant ultramarine to a dazzling white . Conceived as a kind of town square, the exhilarating and expansive canyon-like space extends the public realm into the building. Daylight is diffused by a line of computer-controlled sunshades set just below the glass roof. In a reprise of Alsop's surreal form-making, the atrium contains a small exhibition space housed in an extruded elliptical container – an echo of de Chirico.

Unlike in the United Kingdom, where such an unorthodox piece of architecture would struggle to gain public acceptance, France has a more enlightened approach to the commissioning of buildings. For example, all public buildings over a certain contract value are the subject of an architectural competition, as this was. Architecture and politics are also more closely interwoven, so the expressive quality of Alsop's building is not entirely inappropriate – it is able to be both an extraordinary civic landmark and a flamboyant symbol of regional political identity.

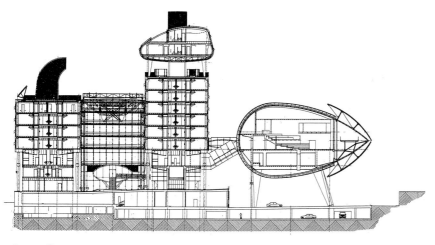

Cross section

Far left The canyon-like atrium at the heart of the *Administratif* is a generous, expansive space articulated by rows of bulbous, X-shaped pilotis supporting the office floors above.

Left The atrium is conceived as a kind of new town square, extending and embracing the public realm. Elevated walkways link the wings of offices. The intense, clinical whiteness of the interior is dazzling. Computer-controlled sunshades set in the roof space diffuse the daylight.

Below The horseshoe-shaped debating chamber, at the plan's centre, is the focus of the *Délibératif*.

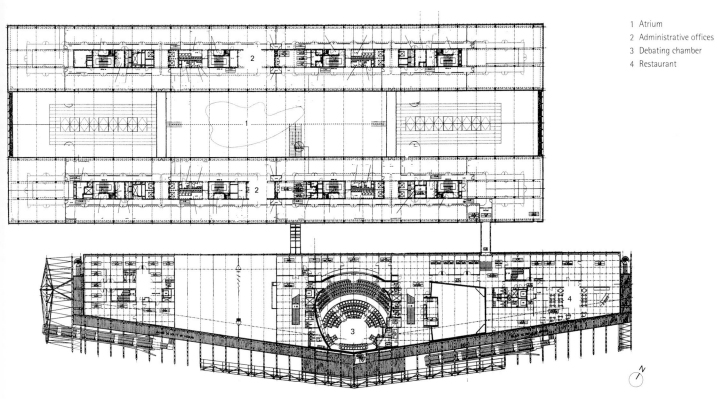

1 Atrium
2 Administrative offices
3 Debating chamber
4 Restaurant

Typical upper-level plan (scale approx. 1:400)

Above The distinctive cigar-shaped form of the *Délibératif* is elevated on sets of splayed legs. White fabric awnings stretched across its ribcage shade the external walkways and reduce heat gain in the chamber.

Right The interior of the debating chamber designed by Andreé Putman. Putman's interiors determinedly ignore the shape of the object they inhabit.

Opposite 'War of the Worlds' in a Marseilles suburb: at times Alsop's futuristic imagery seems disarmingly at odds with its surroundings.

Superstore

- Jeremy Dixon and Edward Jones
- Plymouth, England
- 1995

Above The interlocking meringue peaks of the canopy structure create an invigorating and appropriately nautical new landmark on the edge of Plymouth.

Opposite, above left Perspective of the collage of elements in the landscape. The semicircle of car parking is treated as an external room, its formal geometry emphasized by a serried row of trees along its edge. The site is hemmed in by a motorway and railway line.

Opposite, above right The steel lattice structure of the individual sails that make up the canopy was based on the model of soap film, so that the pre-stressed fabric would accurately follow the surface of the lattice without requiring additional restraint. The hierarchy of structural members – from the trunk-like supports to the more delicate lattices – is clearly and beautifully expressed.

Opposite, below The convoy of sails startlingly invigorates the low-slung volume of the superstore, giving it a bold civic presence.

Out-of-town retailing has spawned its own particular brand of cheap and generally rather nasty architecture. Clusters of lamely decorated sheds surrounded by acres of parking are now an established blot on the British landscape. Most retailers are reluctant to deviate beyond formulaic solutions designed to be plonked on any available site. One exception to these retailers is Sainsbury's, which has a decent track record of attempting to instil its stores with some kind of architectural panache. Aware that good architecture can heighten its corporate profile, Sainsbury's has previously commissioned (among others), Nicholas Grimshaw for a key inner-city store in Camden Town, London, and Lifschutz Davidson (an emerging young British practice) to design a sleekly modern supershed outside Coventry. For this new store in Plymouth, Jeremy Dixon and Edward Jones succeed in elevating the debased supermarket typology into an inventive collage of sculptural elements in the landscape.

The building is located on the eastern edge of Plymouth, on a heart-shaped plot flanked by a circular road system, a railway track and the Plym estuary. Despite its apparent featurelessness, the site overlooks the main motorway into Plymouth, suggesting the potential for a city gateway, which has been inventively exploited by Dixon and Jones. The low-slung, single-storey volume of the supermarket turns its back on the

prevailing winds blowing up the estuary and faces the motorway across a semicircular expanse of parking. Instead of disguising the presence of vehicles, Dixon and Jones treat the parking area as an outdoor room or theatre, emphasizing its formal geometry with a sentinel row of oak trees along the curved perimeter. Service spaces, such as offices, plant, a small tourist office and amenities for the four hundred staff, are also delineated and expressed as discrete components around the sharply articulated supermarket volume. Materially, an elegant functionalism prevails: earthy red-brick textures, Cornish slate and terracotta are set against the svelte, stainless-steel panels of the main entrance façade.

This restrained palette forms a backdrop to the building's most conspicuous element, a long canopy of interlocking paraboloid sails that extends along the main elevation. Part sign, part sculpture, part sheltering arcade, the canopy is constructed from semi-translucent PVC membrane stretched over an armature of fine steel. Conceived by Peter Rice and refined by Martin Manning of Ove Arup & Partners, the sails are supported on tree-like structures, with doubly curving steel lattices (across which the membrane is stretched) cantilevered off a network of branches. The structure's dynamic forms call to mind a schooner in full sail – an appropriately nautical analogy for Plymouth – or a queue of nuns, an effect both delightful and surprising.

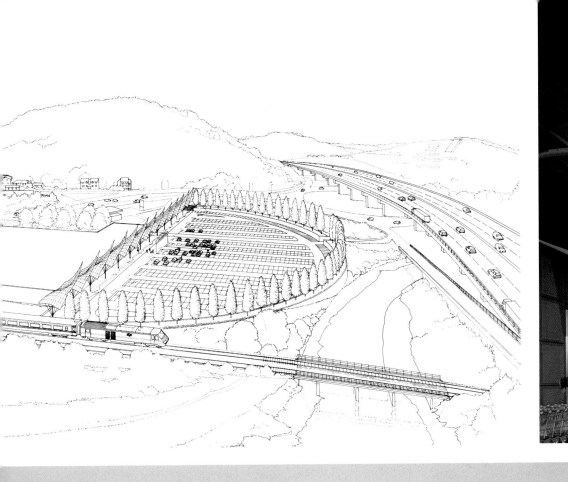

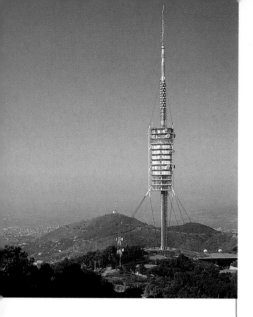

Communications Tower

- Foster and Partners
- Barcelona, Spain
- 1992

Above The Collserola communications mast acts as a visual pivot to the extended city and is executed with an elegance that befits its symbolic role.

Below Site plan. The tower stands on the saddle of the Tibidabo ridge.

Opposite Post-tensioned cables moor the tower in place.

Of all the new buildings and infrastructural projects generated by Barcelona's energetic reinvention of itself for the 1992 Olympic Games, the Collserola communications tower by Norman Foster is one of the few that has the makings of an enduring landmark. Determined that the city should not be surrounded by a miscellaneous collection of communications structures, Pasqual Maragall, then mayor of Barcelona, held a limited competition for a single tower on the saddle of Tibidabo, a dominant ridge that traditionally formed the edge of the city against its northern hinterland.

Foster's aim was to make the tower as slender as possible, and his solution displays an ingenious yet elegant refinement of the most stringent engineering criteria. The mast structure is essentially a colossal 205-metre-tall concrete tube, 4 metres in diameter and stiffened by three steel trusses set 120 degrees to each other in plan. The concrete shaft is topped by a slim steel mast that functions as a television antenna. Lower down the tower, microwave and radio transmitters are located on twelve triangular platforms; a thirteenth at the top of the stack acts as a spectacular viewing terrace. The entire structure, which has to be very stable to project its broadcast accurately, is held in place by post-tensioned Kevlar guys attached in pairs to the trusses.

Below the tower is a large ancillary building that is partly submerged beneath the earth to minimize its impact in the landscape and has a roof that echoes the curve of the ridge.

Both in its prominent location – it is highly visible from all parts of the city – and its technological sophistication, the tower is an appropriate symbol of Barcelona's determination to approach the future with optimism.

N

Site plan

Above The public viewing deck on the thirteenth floor provides breathtaking vistas of Barcelona and the surrounding Catalan landscape.

Below Plan of a typical operations level. Two lifts and a caged staircase run up beside the central shaft.

Above Inside one of the operations levels showing the structural core – a massive concrete support 4 metres in diameter – and one of the three steel trusses set at 120 degrees to the column.

Right From the ground, the tower appears as a heroic structural form. The muscularity of the central support contrasts with the lightness of the steel mesh platforms.

Opposite, left Cross section through the tower and the subterranean ancillary building. Not a great deal has changed from Foster's elegant concept sketch.

Opposite, right Festooned with communications equipment, the tower is an icon of technological progress as well as an expression of civic identity.

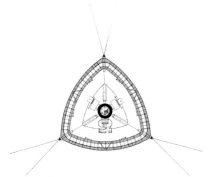

Plan of typical operations level
(scale approx. 1:1000)

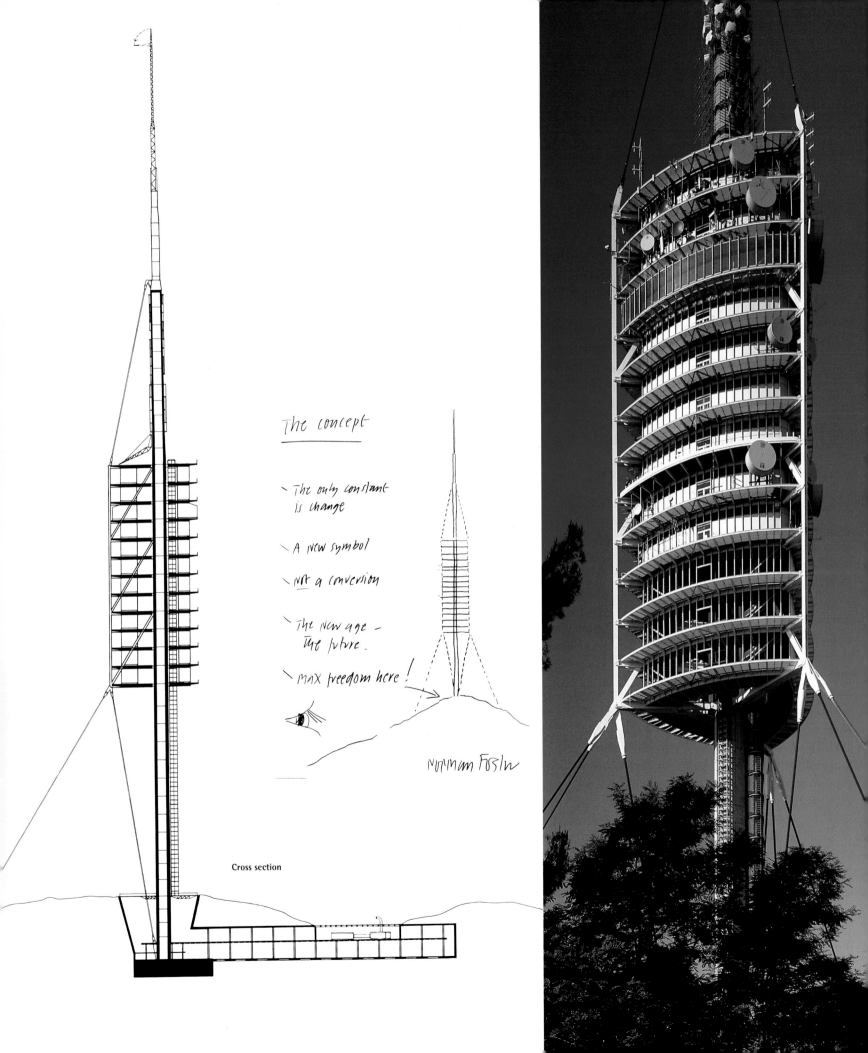

The concept

- The only constant
  is change

- A new symbol

- <u>not</u> a conversion

- The new age -
  the future.

- max freedom here!

Norman Foster

Cross section

Barometer

- Brookes Stacey Randall Fursdon
- London, England
- 1995

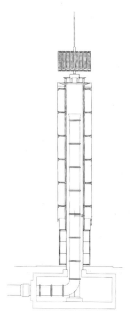

Cross section

Top The sleek, tubular form of the barometer enlivens a dreary London roundabout.

Above The cross section shows how the barometer is constructed around an existing pipe.

Opposite, left Photovoltaic cells on the projecting fins at the top of the structure help to power the barometer mechanism.

In terms of scale and vision the London ring water main, completed in 1995, was a prodigious engineering feat to rival the Victorians. Yet paradoxically, the achievement was totally invisible, buried below the surface of the capital's streets. To mark its completion in a more visible way, Brookes Stacey Randall Fursdon were commissioned by Thames Water to design a landmark tower. Eschewing static monuments, their design takes the form of a giant operational barometer in the middle of a major roundabout in west London.

The device is constructed around an existing surge pipe that relieves pressure on the ring main. The pipe is an imposing structure, 1.5 metres in diameter, rising 15 metres above ground and enclosed in a flush glass cylinder with a series of water jets inserted into the cavity between pipe and cylinder at 2-metre intervals. A barometric monitor translates atmospheric pressure into an electrical signal that controls the water jets.

As the pressure changes, so does the number of nozzles activated, causing the water level in the cylinder to rise and fall; the higher the pressure, the more nozzles are engaged. Water discharged from the nozzles is collected and recycled via pumps and recirculation vessels at the base of the tower, which is protected by a sleek metal casing to deter potential vandalism. The transparent tube is topped by a sculptural row of lightweight fins containing solar cells, which help offset the tower's modest energy requirements.

The water is dyed an intense blue so that the level can be more easily calibrated from a distance and the visual effect of its motion is intensified. At night the core, void and water are illuminated, highlighting the sensual movement of water on the inside face of the cylinder. Part kinetic sculpture, part barometer, part water pipe, this ingenious structure is a stimulating and inspired focal point among dreary surroundings.

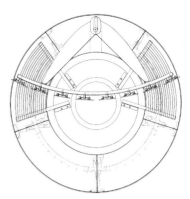

Plan from above

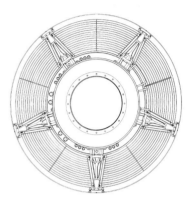

Plan of typical access level

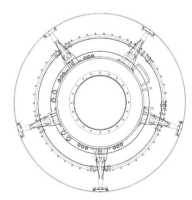

Plan of typical spray ring level

Above Plans of various levels describe the form and operation of the barometer.

European Court of Human Rights

•⌐ Richard Rogers Partnership

•⌐ Strasbourg, France

•⌐ 1995

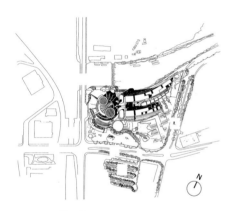

Site plan

Top Undaunted by the potentially overpowering aura of a major European institution, Rogers uses demotic 'industrial' materials (albeit elevated to a certain level of refinement) and reaffirms an uncomplicated enjoyment of the 'poetry of equipment'.

Above The site plans shows how the court occupies a riverside location on the edge of Strasbourg. The campus-like site is given over to a range of somewhat ill-assorted buildings housing other pan-European organizations.

Opposite Junction of the glazed entrance hall and one of the courtroom drums. The curvilinear forms and red components allude to the work of the Russian Constructivists.

Throughout its history Strasbourg has oscillated between French and German possession. After World War II it finally settled into French hands and became an important location for the evolving pan-European organizations of the late 1940s. Among the institutions now based there is the Council of Europe, the supreme body concerned with law, human rights and culture. The many responsibilities the council oversees include the activities of the European Court of Human Rights and the European Commission, the highest courts in Europe.

By the late 1980s, the Court of Human Rights had outgrown its original neo-Corbusian headquarters and plans for a new building were well advanced – to the extent that President Mitterand had been invited to lay the foundation stone– but then an extraordinary volte-face occurred. On reviewing the proposals Mitterand pointedly refused to undertake the ceremony and decreed that the design should be put out to competition, which was eventually won by Richard Rogers.

Rogers's design is intended to be a 'non-monumental monument', a dignified yet accessible expression of jurisprudence in modern European society. The building's component functions are dissected into discrete volumes arranged in a vaguely zoomorphic, tripartite pattern of head, neck and tail. The bug-eyed head of the building consists of two chamfered cylinders linked by an interstitial glass drum. The larger cylinder houses the building's symbolic and functional focus, the European

Court of Human Rights; the smaller space is occupied by the European Commission. Although used only intermittently (the courts sit about one week per month), the chambers represent the set-piece performance spaces around which – in the manner of a theatre – the building revolves.

A narrow neck connected to the bulbous heads contains meeting spaces. Beyond it the entomological overtones give way to nautical ones, as two stepped, parallel office blocks curve languidly along the bank of the River Ill like an ocean liner in full sail. As more emerging nations join the Council of Europe, the office tailpiece can be extended incrementally along the river.

Materials are starkly industrial, accented by scintillating bursts of colour. Bold references to the Russian Contructivism of the Vesnin brothers are apparent in the vivid carmine metal work of the lift shafts, rooftop plant rooms and the delicate spiral escape staircase that clings like an exotic red-wood shaving to the European Commission cylinder. The curving form of the offices also recalls Erich Mendelsohn's sinuous, organic Expressionism.

Rogers' intention to demystify the processes of law is perhaps most potently realized in the pivotal entrance hall that links the two chambers. Instead of repeating the daunting claustrophobia normally associated with law courts, he has created a magically transparent drum full of light, spatial drama and tectonic intricacy.

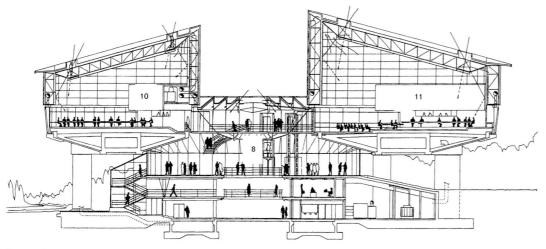

Cross section

1 Direction (administration and documentation)
2 Press hall
3 Cafeteria
4 Kitchen
5 Archives
6 Plant
7 Committee rooms
8 Public entrance hall
9 Offices
10 European Commission
11 Court of Human Rights

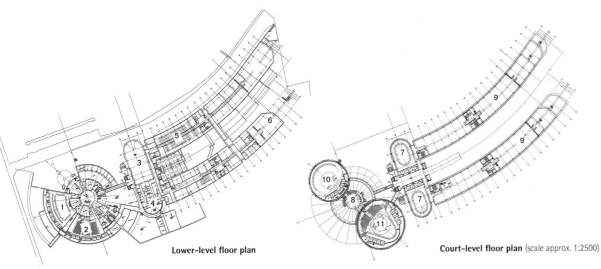

Lower-level floor plan

Court-level floor plan (scale approx. 1:2500)

Opposite, above Cross section through the public hall and courtroom drums.

Opposite, below Enclosed in sleek, stainless-steel panels, the chamfered cylindrical volumes float above the public hall supported by concrete tripod frames.

Left Floor plans demonstrate the zoomorphic quality of the building. The 'bug eyes' of the two courtrooms are connected by a thorax of circulation that leads to a curved body of offices.

Below The pivotal hall with curved stairs leading up to the courtrooms. The transparency of the building aims to reveal the workings of the processes of law at their highest level.

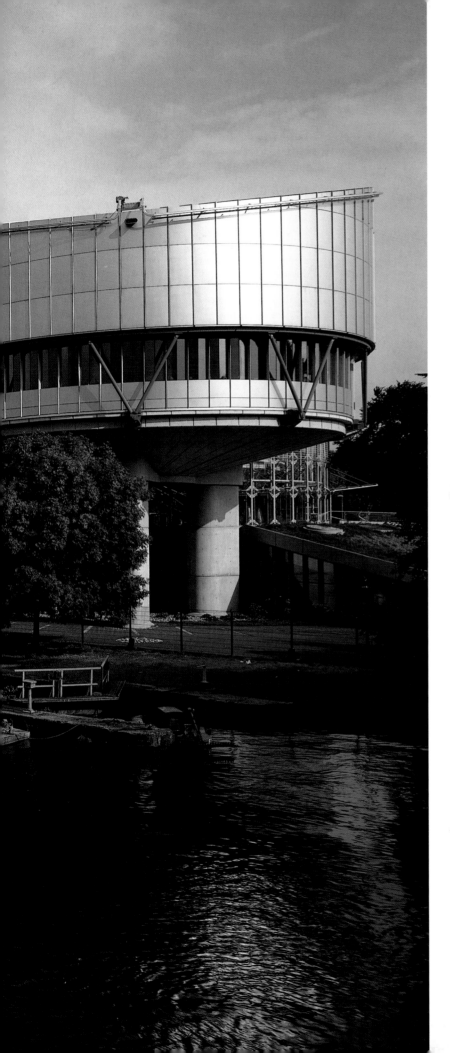

Left The stepped parallel wings of offices curve along the riverside like a languid ocean liner. With its conflation of nautical, industrial and entomological imagery, a major institution is recast into an approachable, legible yet appropriately monumental building. The complex also embodies a degree of energy consciousness: apart from the chambers and one or two other sensitive places, there is no artificial cooling. Equable temperatures are achieved in the double-banked offices by a combination of shading and natural ventilation coupled with the thermal mass of the concrete structure.

Below Rogers' initial concept sketch clearly shows the building's stepped massing and suggests the relationship between the head and the curving tail. As more nations join the Council of Europe, the tail can be extended incrementally.

Following page The spatial and structural drama of the public entrance hall stairs.

Project Information

WESTERN MORNING NEWS HEADQUARTERS, PLYMOUTH
Architect
Nicholas Grimshaw and Partners
Project team Lindy Atkin, Eoin Billings, Paul Grayshon, Nicholas Grimshaw, Andrew Hall, Duncan Jackson, Jonathan Leah, Nicola Macdonald, Christopher Nash, Julian Scanlan, Matthew Seabrook, Mike Waddington, Martin Wood
Structural engineer
Ove Arup & Partners
Services engineer
Cundall Jonston & Partners
Quantity surveyor
Davis Langdon & Everest

NATIONAL GYMNASTICS CENTRE, ALICANTE
Architect Enric Miralles
Project team Enric Miralles, Carme Pinós, Josep Miás, Eva Prats, Rodrigo Prats, Joan Callis, G. M. Godoy, P. Wortham, Francesc Pla, C. Batelli, E. Aymerich, Miquel Lluch, B. Maestenbroeck, Jordi Artigues, Peter Bundgaard, Ricardo Flores, I. Witt
Structural engineer BOMA

IGUS FACTORY, COLOGNE
Architect
Nicholas Grimshaw and Partners
Project team Mark Bryden, Penny Collins, Nicholas Grimshaw, David Harriss, Dorothee Strauss
Structural and services engineer
Whitby & Bird
Quantity surveyor
Davis Langdon & Everest

ALAMILLO BRIDGE, SEVILLE
Architect Calatrava Valls
Structural engineer Calatrava Valls

TRINITY BRIDGE, SALFORD
Architect Calatrava Valls
Project team Santiago Calatrava, Jose Moro, Peter Luty
Associate architect
Dennis Sharp Architects
Structural engineer Calatrava Valls
Consultant engineer Buro Happold
Site engineer Salford City Technical Services Department

EXHIBITION HALL, LINZ
Architect Thomas Herzog and Partners
Project team Thomas Herzog, Hanns Jörg Schrade, Roland Schneider, Arthur Schankula, Klaus Beslmüller, Andrea Heigl, Oliver Mehl
Structural engineer Sailer + Stepan
Services engineer Mathias Bloos

RAC REGIONAL CONTROL CENTRE, BRISTOL
Architect
Nicholas Grimshaw and Partners
Project team Eoin Billings, Mark Bryden, Robert Ellison, Nick Grimshaw, Deborah Jackson, Duncan Jackson, Julian King, Hayley Spurling, Mike Waddington, Martin Wood, Sarah Yabsley
Structural engineer
Alan Baxter Associates
Services engineer Ove Arup & Partners
Quantity surveyor Hanscomb
Landscape consultant Edwards Gale

WILKAHN FACTORY, BAD MUNDER
Architect Thomas Herzog and Partners
Project team Thomas Herzog, Bernd Steigerwald
Associate architects Haag, von Ohlen, Rüffer + Partner, Holger Gestering
Structural engineer
Sailer + Stepan

MUSEUM OF FRUIT, YAMANASHI
Architect Itsuko Hasegawa Atelier
Structural engineer
Ove Arup & Partners, Japan
Services engineer Setsubi Giken

LAW FACULTY, CAMBRIDGE
Architect Foster and Partners
Project team Norman Foster, Spencer de Grey, John Silver, Chris Connell, Michael Jones, Mouzhan Majidi, Giuseppe Boscherini, Angus Campbell, Glenis Fan, Jason Flanagan, Lucy Highton, Ben Marshall, Divya Patel, Kate Peake, Victoria Pike, Austin Relton, Giles Robinson, John Small, Ken Wai, Cindy Walters, Ricarda Zimmerer
Structural engineer
YRM Anthony Hunt Associates
Quantity surveyor
Davis Langdon & Everest
Services engineer YRM Engineers
Landscape consultant
Cambridge Landscape Architects

SECONDARY SCHOOL, VIENNA
Architect Helmut Richter
Project team Helmut Richter, Jakob Dunkl, Gerd Erhartt, Andreas Gerner, Heide Mehring

Structural engineers
Vasko + Partner, Lothar Heinrich
Services engineer Erich Panzhauser

MUSEUM OF GLASS, KINGSWINFORD
Architect Design Antenna
Project team Brent Richards, Robert Dabell
Structural engineer
Dewhurst Macfarlane

CY TWOMBLY GALLERY, HOUSTON
Architect
Renzo Piano Building Workshop
Project team Renzo Piano, Shunji Ishida, Mark Carroll, Michael Palmore, S. Comer, Alison Ewing, Steve Lopez, M. Bassignani
Associate architect
Richard Fitzgerald & Associates
Structural and services engineer
Ove Arup & Partners
Structural engineer
Haynes Whaley Associates
Civil engineer
Lockwood Andrews & Newman

CARTIER FOUNDATION, PARIS
Architect Jean Nouvel, Emmanuel Cattani and Associates
Project team Pierre André Bohnet, Laurence Ininguez, Philippe Mathieu, Viviane Morteau, Guillaume Potet, Steve Ray, Arnaud Villard, Stéphane Robert, Massimo Quendolo
Structural engineer
Ove Arup & Partners
Landscape consultant
Lothar Baumgarten

GLASS HALL, LEIPZIG
Masterplan architect
Von Gerkan Marg and Partners
Architect
Ian Ritchie Architects
Project team Ian Ritchie,
Simon Conolly, Henning Rambow,
Elden Croy, John Randle
Structural engineer IPP
Services engineer
HL Technik
Landscape consultant
Wehberg Lange Eppinger Schmidtke

CITE INTERNATIONALE, LYONS
Architect
Renzo Piano Building Workshop
Project team Renzo Piano,
Paul Vincent, Antoine Chaaya,
Alain Gallisian, Maire Henry,
Charlotte Jackman, Jean Bernard Mothes,
Maria Salerno, Anne Hélène Téménides,
C. Calafell, Michelle Howard,
Ahmed El Jerari, Eric Novel,
Marie Pimmel, J-A Polette,
Bruno Tonfoni, W. Wassal
Associate architect
Curtelin Ricard Bergeret
Landscape consultant Michel Corajoud

UNESCO LABORATORY AND
WORKSHOP, VESIMA
Architect
Renzo Piano Building Workshop
Project team Renzo Piano, Maria
Cattaneo, Flavio Marano, Shunji Ishida,
Massimilino Lusetti, Marco Nouvion,
Mark Carroll, Ottavio di Blasi,
Renzo Venanzio Trufelli,
Maurizio Varratta

Structural engineer P. Costa
Landscape consultant
Michel Desvigne

EXHIBITION HALL, HANOVER
Architect Thomas Herzog and Partners
Project team Thomas Herzog,
Hanns Jörg Schrade, Michael Volz,
Roland Schneider
Structural engineer
Schlaich Bergermann
Services engineer HL Technik

BRITISH PAVILION, SEVILLE
Architect
Nicholas Grimshaw and Partners
Project team Eion Billings, Paul Cook,
Mark Fisher, Nick Grimshaw, Duncan
Jackson, Andrew Hall, Rosemary Latter,
John Martin, Christopher Nash,
Julian Scanlan, Rob Watson
Structural and environmental
engineer Ove Arup & Partners
Quantity surveyor
Davis Langdon & Everest
Water feature consultant
William Pye Partnership

MICROELECTRONICS PARK,
DUISBURG
Architect Foster and Partners
Project team Norman Foster,
David Nelson, Stefan Behling,
Christopher Allercamp,
Sandy Bailey, Mary Bowman,
Georg Gewers, Serina Heijas,
Andre Poitier, Achim Weinmann,
Paul Kalkhoven, Micheal Wurzel,
Andreas Wolf, Maik Butler, Mark Bax,
Jeff Brooks, Caroline Brown, Glenis Fan,
Matteo Fantoni, Helen Goodland,

Caroline Hislop, Reinhard Joecks,
Stuart Latham, Alistair MacMillan,
Jons Messedat, Reinhold Schmaderer,
B. Shrank, Andrew Stuart, Moritz Theder,
Andreas Weinmann, Andrjez Wronkowski,
Martin Wäschle
Structural engineer
Reinhold Meyer
Services engineers Erbert Ingenieure,
J. Roger Preston & Partners, Rud Otto
Meyer, Kaiser Bautechnik
Quantity surveyor and project
management Diederichs & Partner

INLAND REVENUE HEADQUARTERS,
NOTTINGHAM
Architect Michael Hopkins and Partners
Project team Michael Hopkins,
Ian Sharratt, William Taylor,
Peter Romaniuk, Pamela Bate,
Brendan Phelan, Peter Cartwright,
Stephen Macbean, Ernest Sim Fasanya,
Brian Reynolds, Catherine Martin,
Charles Walker, Guni Suri, Lynn Bacher,
Jonathan Knight, Nathan Barr,
Jason Cooper, Lydia Haack, Max Connop,
Russell Baylis, Paul Cutler, Simon Fraser,
Annabel Judd, Alan Jones, Chris Wright,
Cari Wallet, Carol Painter
Structural and services engineer
Ove Arup & Partners
Quantity surveyor
Turner & Townsend

CHANNEL FOUR HEADQUARTERS,
LONDON
Architect Richard Rogers Partnership
Project team Laurie Abbot, Yasmin Al-
Ani, Helen Brunskill, Oliver Collignon,
Mark Collins, Mark Darbon, Mike Davies,
Jane Donnelly, Mike Fairbrass,

Florian Fischötter, Marco Goldschmied,
Philip Gumuchdjian, Jackie Hands,
Bjork Haraldsdottir, Stig Larsen,
Carmel Lewin, Stephen Light, Avtar Lotay,
Steve Martin, Andrew Morris,
Louise Palomba, Elizabeth Parr,
Kim Quazi, Susan Rice,
Richard Rogers, Daniel Sibert,
Stephen Spence, Kinna Stallard,
Graham Stirk, Yuli Toh,
Alec Vassiliades, Martin White,
Adrian Williams, Megan Williams,
John Young
Structural engineer
Ove Arup & Partners
Services engineer YRM Engineers
Quantity surveyor
The Wheeler Group Consultancy
Acoustic consultants
Sandy Brown Associates
Landscape consultants
Rendel + Branch

BRACKEN HOUSE, LONDON
Architect Michael Hopkins and Partners
Project team Michael Hopkins,
John Pringle, David Selby, Robin Snell,
Bill Dunster, Arif Mehmood, Patrick Nee,
Colin Muir, Andrew Barnett, Boon Yang
Sim, Helena Webster, Emma Nsugbe,
Alessandro Calafati, Ernest Fasanya,
Emma Adams, Charles Webster,
Loretta Gentilini, Sanja Polescuk,
Maki Kuwayama, Mike Eleftheriades,
Neno Kezic, Tommaso del Buono,
Steve Piponides, Nicholas Boyarsky,
Gail Halvorsen, Amir Sanei,
Robert Bishop, Fiona Thompson,
Eva Jensen, Margaret Leong, Nick Malby,
Pippa Nissen, Joao Passanha,
Oriel Prizeman, Sundeep Singh Bhamra,

Ameer Bin Tahir, Chris Thurlbourne,
Jim Dunster
Structural and services engineer
Ove Arup & Partners
Quantity surveyor
Northcroft Neighbour & Nicholson
Acoustic consultant
Arup Acoustics

KABUKI-CHO TOWER, TOKYO
Architect Richard Rogers Partnership
Project team Laurie Abbott,
Maxine Campbell, Michael Davies,
Florian Eames, Michael Elkan,
Stuart Forbes-Waller,
Marco Goldschmeid, Horishi Hibio,
Eric Holt, Miyuli Kurihara,
Stig Larsen, John Lowe, Richard Rogers,
Atsushi Sasa, Kyoko Tomioka,
Yoshi Uchiyama, Christopher Wan,
Benjamin Warner, John Young
Associate architect Architect 5
Structural engineer
Umezawa Design Office
Services engineer ES Associates

CARRE D'ART, NIMES
Architect Foster and Partners
Project team Norman Foster, Wendy
Foster, Robin Partington, Max Neal,
Nic Bailey, Andrew Birds, Nicholas
Eldridge, Martin Francis, Paul Jones,
Serge Belet, Arnault de Bussière,
Garnet Geissler, Michael Haste,
Richard Hawkins, Edward Hutchison,
Huat Lim, David Morley,
Hartwig Schneider, Martin Webler,
Sabiha Foster, Ken Shuttleworth,
David Nelson, Graham Phillips,
Robin Partington, Rodney Uren,

Paul Kalkhoven, Alex Reid,
Arthur Branthwaite, Chris Eisner,
Tim Quick, John Small, Chris Abel,
Ruth Conroy, Katherine Delpino,
Pascal Desplanques, Shaun Earle,
Bertrand Feinte, Lulie Fisher,
Jean Pierre Genevois, Bruce Graham,
Michael Jones, Alexander Lamboley,
Eddie Lamptey, John McFarland,
Sophie Mears, Jesper Neilson,
Irene Pham, Victoria Pike, Etienne
Renault, Joel Rutten, Kriti Siderakis,
Ken Wai, Cindy Walters, Louisa Williams
Structural engineer
Ove Arup & Partners
Services engineer OTH
Quantity surveyor Thorne Wheatley

PORT RESTORATION, GENOA
Architect
Renzo Piano Building Workshop
Project team Renzo Piano,
Shunji Ishida, Emanuela Baglietto,
Giorgio Bianchi, Paolo Bodega,
Mark Carroll, Olaf de Nooyer,
Donald Hart, Claudio Manfredo,
Vittorio Tolu, Renzo Venanzio Truffelli
Structural engineer
Ove Arup & Partners
Services engineer Manens Intertecnica
Naval engineer Cetena
Quantity surveyor STED

CENTURY TOWER, TOKYO
Architect Foster and Partners
Project team Norman Foster,
David Nelson, Ken Shuttleworth,
Mark Bramhall, Hing Chan,
Tom Politowicz, Alf Seeling,
Armstrong Yakubu, Chris Seddon,

Hans Brouwer, Andy Miller, Kent
Lui, Hiromi Uno
Structural engineer
Ove Arup & Partners
Services engineer
J. Roger Preston & Partners
Quantity surveyor
Northcroft Neighbour & Nicholson

KANSAI AIRPORT, OSAKA
Architect
Renzo Piano Building Workshop
Project team Renzo Piano,
Noriaki Okabe, Jean-François Blassel,
Ariel Chavela, Ivan Corte, Kenneth Fraser,
Robert S. Garlipp, Marion Goerdt,
Greg Hall, Kohji Hirano, Akira Ikegami,
Shunji Ishida, Amanda Johnson,
Christopher Kelly, Tetsuya Kimura,
Stig Larsen, Jean Lelay, Ken McBryde,
Takeshi Miyazaki, Shin'ichi Nakaya,
Norio Takuta, Taichi Tomuro,
Olivier Touraine, Mark Turpin,
Masami Yamada, Hiroshi Yamaguchi,
Tatsuya Yamaguchi, Alexandre Autin,
Geoffrye Cohen, Anahita Golzari, Barnaby
Gunning, Gunther Hastrich, Masahiro
Horie, Ikuko Kubo, Simone Medin,
Keisuke Miyake, Sandro Montaldo,
Shin'ichiro Mukai, Kamran Afshar,
Koung Nyunt, Stefan Oehler,
Tim O'Sullivan, Patrizia Persia,
Milly Rossato, Randy Shields,
Takehim Takagawa, Takuo Ueno,
Yoshiko Ueno, Kiyomi Uezano,
Jean-Marc Weill, Tetsuo Yamakoshi,
Taichi Tomuro, Shin Kano, Aki Shimizu
Associate architect
Nikken Sekkei
Structural and services engineer
Ove Arup & Partners

WATERLOO STATION
INTERNATIONAL TERMINAL, LONDON
Architect
Nicholas Grimshaw and Partners
Project team Rowena Bate, Ingrid Bille,
Conal Campbell, Garry Colligan, Geoff
Crowe, Florian Eames, Alex Fergusson,
Nick Grimshaw, Sarah Hare, Eric Jaffres,
Ursula Heinemann, Doug Keys, David
Kirkland, Chris Lee, Colin Leisk,
Jan Mackie, Julian Maynard, Neven Sidor,
Ulriche Seifutz, Will Stevens,
George Stowell, Andrew Whalley,
Robert Wood, Sara Yabsley,
Richard Walker
Structural engineers
YRM Anthony Hunt Associates, Cass
Hayward & Partners, Tony Gee & Partners,
British Rail Network Civil Engineers,
Sir Alexander Gibb & Partners
Quantity surveyor
Davis Langdon & Everest

MARSEILLES AIRPORT
Architect Richard Rogers Partnership
Project team Peter Barber,
Pierre Botschi, Tim Colquhoun,
Mike Davies, Marco Goldschmeid,
Lennart Grut, Enrique Hermoso-Lera,
Oliver Kühn, Swantje Kühn,
Michael McNamara,
Gregoris Patslosavvis, Kim Quazi,
Richard Rogers, John Smith, John Young
Associate architects Atelier 9, ETA
Structural engineer
Ove Arup & Partners

LYONS AIRPORT TGV STATION
Architect Calatrava Valls
Project team Santiago Calatrava,

Sébastien Memet
Engineer Calatrava Valls
Quantity surveyor
Cabinet Voutay

STUTTGART AIRPORT
Architect
Von Gerkan Marg and Partners
Project team Meinhard von Gerkan,
Karsten Brauer, Michael Dittmer,
Otto Dorn, Marion Ebeling,
Rudolf Henning, Antje Lucks,
Marion Mews, Hans-Heinrich Möller,
Klaus-Heinrich Petersen, Peter Sembritzki,
Horst Thimian, Christel Timm-Schwarz,
Tuyen Tran-Viet, Arturo Buchholz-Berger,
Edeltraut Grimmer, Gabriele Hagermeister,
Berthold Kiel, Uwe Pörksen,
Stefan Rimpf, Hitoshi Ueda
Structural engineer
Weidleplan Consulting

FERRY TERMINAL, HAMBURG
Architect William Alsop Architects
Associate architect
me di um Architects
Project team William Alsop,
Jan Störmer, Holger Jaedicke,
Gabriela Langosch, Pierre Andre Bohnet,
James Brearley, Barbara Jentz-Koska,
John McCarthy, Katrin Wolke
Structural engineer
Ove Arup & Partners
Services engineer
Sellhorn Inegenieurbüro

EURALILLE STATION, LILLE
Architect SNCF Architects
Project architect Jean-Marie Duthilleul

Structural engineer
Ove Arup & Partners
Project team Andrew Allsop,
Maki Banfi, Chris Barder, Paula Beever,
Sean Billings, Simon Cardwell, Brian Duck,
Ed Forwood, Lesley Graham,
Sophie Le Bourva, Alistair Lenczner,
Alain Marcetteau, Sean McGinn,
Craig McQueen, Chris Murgatroyd,
Strachan Mitchell, Neil Noble,
Jane Peel-Cross, Peter Rice,
Adrian Robinson, Lizzie Sironic,
Darren Sri-Tharan, Jane Wernick,
Derek Woodcraft
Cladding consultant RFR

STANSTED AIRPORT
Architect Foster and Partners
Project team Norman Foster,
Spencer de Grey, Chubby Chhabra,
John Silver, Alex Reid, Winston Shu,
Paul Kalkhoven, Arthur Branthwaite,
John Small, Chris Eisner, Ram Ahronov,
Edward Hutchison, Mary Thum,
Brynley Dyer, Steve Martin,
Moujan Majidi, Camille Olsen,
Richard Holyoak, Ian Norbury,
Valerie Lark, Michael Haste, Jan Krarup,
Tobias Fusban, Tony Smith,
Andrew Thompson, Mike Elkan,
Chris Grech, Mike McColl, Michael Jones,
Giuseppe Boscherini, Mike Jeliffe
Associate architect
British Airports Advisory Consultancy
Structural engineer
Ove Arup & Partners
Quantity surveyors
BAA & Beard Dove/Needleman,
Currie & Brown
Landscape consultant
Adrian Lismey

REGIONAL GOVERNMENT CENTRE,
MARSEILLES
Architect William Alsop Architects
Project team William Alsop,
Francis Graves, Stephen Pimbley,
Peter Angrave, Xauvier D'Alençon,
Sybil Diot-Lamige, John Kember,
Harvey Male, Geoffrey Powis,
Peter Strudwick, George Tsoutsos,
Nicki van Oosten, Gary Taylor
Structural engineer
Ove Arup & Partners International
Quantity surveyor Hanscomb
Bureau d'étude OTH Mediterranée

SUPERSTORE, PLYMOUTH
Architect Jeremy Dixon.Edward Jones
Project team Jeremy Dixon,
Edward Jones, Gordon Cousins, A. Bow,
Mickey Mahava, José Esteves de Matos,
Pascal Madoc Jones, Stuart McKnight
Associate architect
Elseworth Sykes Partnership
Structural engineer
Ove Arup & Partners
Civil and structural engineer
Ernest Green Partnership
Services engineer
Silcock Dawson & Partners
Quantity surveyor
Henry Riley & Son
Landscape consultant
Gillespies

COMMUNICATIONS TOWER,
BARCELONA
Architect Foster and Partners
Project team Norman Foster,
Ken Shuttleworth, Robin Partington,
Mark Bramhall, Mark Sparrowhawk,

Jurgen Willen
Structural engineer
Ove Arup & Partners
Associate structural engineer CAST
Quantity surveyor
Davis Langdon & Everest

BAROMETER, LONDON
Architect
Brooks Stacey Randall Fursdon
Project team Andrew Fursdon,
Paul Voysey, Simon Innes
Concept Damian O'Sullivan, Tania Doufa
Structural engineer SMP Atelier One

EUROPEAN COURT OF HUMAN
RIGHTS, STRASBOURG
Architect Richard Rogers Partnership
Project team Laurie Abbott,
Peter Angrave, Eike Becker,
Mike Davies, Elliot Boyd, Karin Egge,
Marco Goldschmeid, Pascale Gibon,
Lennart Grut, Ivan Harbour, Amarajit
Kalsi, Sze-King Kan, Carmel Lewin,
Avtar Lotay, John Lowe, Louise Palomba,
Richard Rogers, Pascale Rousseau,
Yuli Toh, Sarah Tweedie, Andrew Tyley,
Yoshiyuki Uchiyama, John Young
Site architect
Atelier d'Architecture Claude Bucher
Structural and services engineer
Ove Arup & Partners
Quantity surveyor
Thorne Wheatley Associates
Landscape consultants
David Jarvis Associates, Dan Kiley
Lighting consultant
Lighting Design Partnership
Acoustic consultants Sound Research
Laboratories, Commins Ingemansson

Architects' Biographies

WILL ALSOP

Born in 1947 in Northampton, Alsop studied at the Architectural Association in London. From 1973 he spent periods in the studios of Maxwell Fry, Cedric Price and Roderick Ham. He established his own practice in 1980 and in 1990 went into partnership with German architect Jan Störmer, who was a founding partner in me di um Architects in Hamburg. Their first major project was the ferry terminal for Hamburg's dockside, followed by a competition-winning government headquarters for the Bouche du Rhône region in Marseilles (1994). Alsop's approach to design initially emerges through painting, a medium that allows him to explore the essence of a concept in a free-flowing way and gives rise to idiosyncratic yet ebullient forms. Having parted company with Störmer, Alsop is currently working on his own; recent projects include the Crossrail platform at Paddington Station in London and studies for Blackfriars and Hungerford Bridges, also in London.

BROOKES STACEY RANDALL FURSDON

The London-based practice Brookes Stacey Randall Fursdon was established in 1987. It was founded by Alan Brookes, who was born 1939; the other three partners are Michael Stacey (born 1958), Nik Randall (born 1958) and Andrew Fursdon (born 1957). All trained at the Liverpool School of Architecture. The practice has a reputation for refined modern buildings that display a high level of technical skill; it also specializes in the

design of the building envelope and product/component design. Recent projects include the refurbishment of London's East Croydon Station (1992), the conversion of a penthouse shell into a private flat for musician Chris Lowe of the Pet Shop Boys (1996) and the Thames Tower, an environmentally responsive public barometer in west London (1995).

SANTIAGO CALATRAVA

Born in Benimamet, Spain, in 1951, Calatrava studied architecture at the Valencia School of Architecture from 1969 to 1975, and later studied civil engineering at the Swiss Federal Institute of Technology, ETH, Zurich, before setting up offices there in 1981. As both an architect and an engineer he has designed a number of civil engineering structures as well as buildings, reviving a design tradition that emphasizes the production of dynamic structural forms as a means of aesthetic expression. Major projects include the Bach de Roda Bridge, Barcelona (1987), Stadelhofen Railway Station, Zurich (1990), Alamillo Bridge, Seville (1992), Kuwait Pavilion, Seville (1992), and the Montjuïc Communications Tower, Barcelona (1992). More recently he completed the Lyon Airport TGV Station (1994) and a vast exhibition hall at Santa Cruz in Tenerife (1996), and has begun work on a museum addition in Wisconsin, USA.

DESIGN ANTENNA

Design Antenna was set up in 1992 by Brent Richards. Born in London in 1954, Richards studied architecture at Aston University and Plymouth School of Architecture. Between 1985 and 1991 he

was director of architecture in Le-Plan Design Consultancy, as well as teaching at the Polytechnic of Central London, Kingston University and Central Saint Martins College of Art & Design in London. Broadfield House Glass Museum (1995) is currently the largest all-glass structure in the world; it has caught the imagination of the public and recieved several design awards. Since 1996 Brent Richards has been the dean of London's Central Saint Martin's, and is currently working on the National Glass Museum in England's West Midlands.

JEREMY DIXON EDWARD JONES

The Jeremy Dixon.Edward Jones partnership is based on a working relationship that dates back to their student days at London's Architectural Association, where they graduated in 1963. In 1972, they won first prize for an international competition for Northamptonshire County Offices. After working for Alison and Peter Smithson and the Milton Keynes Development Corporation, Jeremy Dixon has been in private practice since 1977, building a number of distinctive urban housing projects in London. His St Mark's Road housing in Maida Vale (1980) and Dudgeon's Wharf on the Isle of Dogs (1988) sensitively married historical and modern traditions. Since 1983, Dixon has been engaged in designing the Royal Opera House extension in Covent Garden, in association with Building Design Partnership. He also designed the coffee shop (1982) and restaurant (1984) at the Tate Gallery in London. In 1990 Edward Jones completed a competition–winning scheme for Missussauga City Hall

in Canada. Recent projects by the partnership include a gallery for the Henry Moore Foundation in Leeds (1993), student housing for Robert Gordon University in Aberdeen (1994) and a superstore for the Sainsbury's chain in Plymouth (1994).

NORMAN FOSTER

Born in 1935 in Manchester, educated at the University of Manchester and Yale University, Foster was a founder member – with his wife, Wendy, and Richard and Su Rogers – of Team 4 in 1963. In 1967 he established Foster Associates, now Foster and Partners, which has evolved into a highly successful international practice. Major projects include the headquarters for Willis Faber Dumas in Ipswich (1975), the Sainsbury Centre for Visual Arts in Norwich (1978), the Hongkong and Shanghai Bank (1985), Stansted Airport (1990) and Century Tower in Tokyo (1991). The practice has recently been involved in the design of a new airport at Chek Lap Kok for Hong Kong, and in 1997 completed Europe's tallest building, the new Commerzbank headquarters in Frankfurt. A leading exponent of technological innovation in architecture, Foster is also deeply concerned with detailing and craftsmanship. His forms and details consciously refer to the world of machinery, with a beauty arising from precise engineering calculations, as in aircraft and industrial design.

NICHOLAS GRIMSHAW

Nicholas Grimshaw was born in 1939 and studied architecture at the Architectural Association in London. Since 1965 he has been in private practice, initially in partnership with Terry Farrell and latterly with his own practice Nicholas Grimshaw and Partners, established in 1980. Grimshaw is among a leading group of British architects whose work continues a tradition of buildings that explore engineering values, yet his technological approach is firmly rooted in humanity. Since the mid-1980s, he has completed a series of major buildings, including the Financial Times Print Works (1988), a supermarket and housing in Camden Town, north London (1990), and the British Pavilion for Seville Expo (1992), an innovative prototype that advances the argument for an ecologically progressive and responsive architecture. Recent projects include a new headquarters for the Western Morning News in Plymouth (1993), the International Terminal at Waterloo Station in London (1993), and the Berlin Stock Exchange (due for completion in 1998).

ITSUKO HASEGAWA
Born in 1941, Itsuko Hasegawa studied architecture at Kanto Gakuin University in Tokyo, graduating in 1964. From 1965 to 1969 she worked in the office Kiyonori Kikutake, then spent nine years at the Tokyo Institute of Technology, initially as a research student and subsequently as an assistant in the studio of Kazuo Shinohara. In 1979 she set up her own practice in Tokyo. Her work combines a sophisticated approach to technology through the use of computers for exploring and modelling building form, with a highly poetic handling of light and space. Major projects include the Shonandai Cultural Centre, Fujisawa

(1990), Sumida Culture Factory, Tokyo (1992), Oshima Machi Picture Book Museum, Oshima (1992) and the extraordinary Museum of Fruit at Yamanashi (1996).

THOMAS HERZOG
Born in 1941 in Munich, Thomas Herzog studied architecture at the Technical University there. Since 1972 he has been active in practice, initially in collaboration with Verena Herzog-Loibl and more recently in partnership (since 1994) with Hanns Jörg Schrade. Herzog is interested not only in the design of buildings but in the development of renewable energy sources and sustainable building products. In 1995 he drafted the European Charter for Solar Energy and Planning, which, supported by the European Commission, set new objectives for energy use in architecture, planning, product development, materials and supply systems. Herzog's buildings are a consistently thoughtful resolution of functional, aesthetic and ecological concerns. His recent projects include a factory extension for the furniture manufacturer Wilkahn at Bad Munder (1993) and two exhibition buildings, in Hanover (1996) and Linz (1994).

MICHAEL HOPKINS
Born in 1935 in Poole, England, Michael Hopkins trained at the Architectural Association between 1959 and 1962. He subsequently worked with Leonard Manassah and Partners (1963–65), Tom Hancock (1966–68) and Foster Associates (1969–75). In 1976 he established Michael Hopkins and Partners in London. With his wife and partner, Patty, Hopkins

has designed some of the most memorable and iconic buildings in England, among them the dramatic tented structures of the Schlumberger Research Laboratories in Cambridge (1985) and the Mound Stand at Lord's Cricket Ground (1987). Since designing their own house in Hampstead (1976) the Hopkins have always explored and exploited the potential of technology, but recently have sought a more subtle fusion of traditional materials and contemporary design, seen in the redevelopment of Bracken House (1991), the new Opera House at Glyndebourne (1994) and a new headquarters for the Inland Revenue in Nottingham (1995). In 1994 the Hopkins were only the second husband–and–wife partnership (after Charles and Ray Eames) to be jointly awarded the RIBA Royal Gold Medal for Architecture.

ENRIC MIRALLES
Enric Miralles was born in 1955 in Barcelona and studied architecture there, graduating in 1978 from the Escuela Tecnica Superior de Arquitectura. In 1984 he established his own practice in Barcelona, where he currently works in partnership with Benedetta Tagliabue Miralles, following successful collaborations with Helio Piñon and Albert Viaplana and, perhaps most notably, with Carme Pinós. Rejecting historical and regional architectural models and traditions, he creates highly fragmented, complex buildings that are passionate expressions of a radical reinterpretation of Modernism. Recent work includes the Igualada Cemetery near Barcelona (1991), the Olympic

archery ranges and Icaria Avenue pergolas (both built for the 1992 Barcelona Games) and the National Gymnastics Centre in Alicante (1993).

JEAN NOUVEL
Jean Nouvel was born in 1945 in Fumel, France. He trained at the Ecole Nationale Supérieure des Beaux Arts, and in 1972 obtained his diploma as an architect. A socialist and early starter – at twenty-three he was already responsible for the construction of eighty apartments in Neuilly – Nouvel's career began to attract international attention with his design for the Institut du Monde Arabe, Paris (1987). A tautly honed sliver of a building on the edge of the Seine, with intricate, mechanized versions of traditional *mashrabiya* screen walls, it demonstrates a poetic yet rigorous application of technology. This approach has been refined through a succession of major (mostly French) projects, including the 'Némausus' housing block in Nîmes (1987), a spa hotel in Dax (1992), the refurbishment of Lyons's opera house (1993) and the Cartier Foundation in Paris (1994). In 1988 Nouvel set up in partnership with Emanual Cattani; the practice's most recent completed project was a department store for the Galeries Lafayette in Berlin (1996).

RENZO PIANO
Renzo Piano was born in Genoa in 1937 and studied at the Milan Politecnico, where he later taught between 1965 and 1968. In 1970 he established a partnership with Richard Rogers and undertook a number of commissions in Italy and England, most notably the

radical, competition-winning design for the Pompidou Centre (1977), which took the form of a 'cultural machine' inserted into the centre of Paris. After parting company with Rogers, Piano established Renzo Piano Building Workshop, based in Genoa. Although he has continued the structural and technological experiments of Pompidou, he has applied them in a wider range of social, participatory and ecological programmes, such as the residential quarter in Corciano, near Perugia (1982) and a Kanak cultural centre in New Caledonia (currently under construction). Recent work includes a new football stadium at Bari built for the 1990 World Cup, Kansai Airport in Osaka Bay (1994) and the redevelopment of Potsdamer Platz in Berlin.

PETER RICE

Born in Ulster in 1935, Peter Rice studied engineering at Queen's University Belfast and at Imperial College in London. In 1956 he started work with the distinguished engineering practice of Ove Arup & Partners, becoming a director in 1978 and remaining with the firm until his death in 1992. With Ian Ritchie and Martin Francis he was also a partner in the Paris-based architectural and engineering practice Rice Francis Ritchie (RFR), set up in 1982. Rice's poetic invention, coupled with his rigorous mathematical and philosophical logic, made him one of the most sought-after and inspirational engineers of recent times. His list of credits includes most of this century's greatest structural feats: Jørn Utzon's Sydney Opera House, the Pompidou Centre in Paris (1977), the Lloyd's Building in London (1984) and

Stansted Airport (1991). In 1992 he was awarded the RIBA Royal Gold Medal for Architecture, a rare accolade for an engineer. His mentor, the brilliant Danish engineer Ove Arup, had been a previous recipient.

HELMUT RICHTER

Helmut Richter was born in 1941 and began his architectural education at the Technical University in Graz. After graduating in 1968, he undertook post-graduate study in Paris and at UCLA in Los Angeles. In 1971 he returned to Paris to teach architecture at the Ecole Supérieure des Beaux Arts and later established his current practice in Vienna in 1977. From his early experimentation with mechanical furniture (1968), Richter has sought to apply technology to architecture in a functionally rigorous manner, while developing an increasingly refined sensibility that combines bold forms with material lightness and transparency. His seamless, crystalline school in a Viennese suburb (1995) also manifests his concern with energy use and environmental control.

IAN RITCHIE

Ian Ritchie was born in 1947 in Hove, England. He trained at the Liverpool School of Architecture (1965-68) and then at the Polytechnic of Central London (1970-72). From 1972 to 1976 Ritchie worked for Foster Associates, where he was involved in the design of the seminal Willis Faber and Dumas offices (1975) and the Sainsbury Centre for the Visual Arts at the University of East Anglia (1978). He then worked independently in Paris before setting up

Chrysalis architects with Michael Dowd and Alan Stanton (1979-81). In 1982 he became a director of Rice Francis Ritchie, (RFR) with Peter Rice and Martin Francis, based in Paris; he also established Ian Ritchie Architects in London. Ritchie's work crosses the disciplines of architecture and engineering, as the adventurous design of his Eagle Rock house (1983) reveals. He has completed housing in London's Docklands (1988) and (with RFR) collaborated with Adrien Fainsilber on the design of three huge greenhouses for the Cité des Sciences et de l'Industrie at the Parc de la Villette in Paris (1986). The structures used newly developed glass-hanging techniques. His most recent project is a vast exhibition hall for Leipzig's trade fair site (1996), with Von Gerkan Marg.

RICHARD ROGERS

Richard Rogers was born in Florence in 1933 and educated at the Architectural Association, London, and Yale University. With his first wife, Su, Rogers formed Team 4 with Norman and Wendy Foster in 1963. The practice's first work was the innovative Reliance Controls Factory at Swindon (1966), an embryonic High Tech building that received considerable attention. Following the dissolution of Team 4, Rogers set up in partnership with the Italian architect Renzo Piano, and established an international reputation with the Pompidou Centre (1977). With its dramatically exposed structure and services and highly flexible interior, the Pompidou represented an avant-garde technological sensibility that has been progressively refined to embrace contemporary preoccupations

with ecology, sustainability and urbanism. In 1977 Rogers founded the Richard Rogers Partnership with John Young, Marco Goldschmied and Mike Davies. The group's challenging and controversial buildings include the Lloyds Building in the City of London (1984), the conversion of Billingsgate Fish Market into dealing rooms (1988), a new headquarters for Channel 4 (1994) and the European Court of Human Rights in Strasbourg (1995). The partnership has recently won a competition to redevelop London's South Bank Centre, a scheme that drew on experience gained in masterplanning the Potsdamer Platz in Berlin and the Lu Jia business district in China.

VON GERKAN MARG AND PARTNERS

Meinhard von Gerkan was born in Riga, Lithuania, in 1935, and moved to Germany in 1945. He studied physics and law at the University of Hamburg and architecture at the Technical University of Berlin and the Technical University of Braunschweig, qualifying in 1964. Since 1965 he has been based in Hamburg, in partnership with Volkwin Marg. Their practice developed rapidly after winning a number of competitions, and has become one of Germany's leading architectural firms. Their approach is characterized by a conscientious and pragmatic analysis of function, local environment and topography that avoids preconceived formal solutions. Notable recent projects include new airport terminals for Stuttgart (1995) and Hamburg (1993) and the masterplanning and design of Leipzig's vast Neue Messe trade fair complex (1996).

Select Bibliography

Bill Addis, *The Art of the Structural Engineer*, Artemis: London, 1994

Reyner Banham, *The Architecture of the Well-tempered Environment*, second edition, The Architectural Press: London, 1984

Sophia and Stefan Behling, *Sol Power*, Prestel: Munich, 1996

Leonardo Benevolo, *The European City*, Blackwell: Oxford 1993

Peter Buchanan, *Renzo Piano Building Workshop Complete Works Vol 1*, Phaidon: London, 1993

Peter Buchanan, *Renzo Piano Building Workshop Complete Works Vol 2*, Phaidon: London, 1995

Richard Burdett, ed., *Richard Rogers Partnership, Works and Projects*, The Monacelli Press: New York, 1996

Andrea Compagno, *Intelligent Glass Facades*, Birkäuser: Basel, 1995

William J. R. Curtis, *Modern Architecture Since 1900*, third edition, Phaidon: London, 1996

Cynthia C. Davidson, ed., *Anywise*, MIT Press: Cambridge, 1996

Colin Davies, *High Tech Architecture*, Thames and Hudson: London, 1988

David Dunster, ed., *Arups on Engineering*, Ernst & Sohn: Berlin, 1996

John Farmer, *Green Shift - Towards a Green Sensibility in Architecture*, Butterworth Architecture: Oxford, 1996

Kenneth Frampton, *Modern Architecture - a Critical History*, second edition, Thames and Hudson: London, 1990

Diane Ghirardo, *Architecture after Modernism*, Thames and Hudson: London, 1996

Mark Girouard, *Cities and People*, Yale University Press: Newhaven, 1985

Robert Harbison, *Creatures from the Mind of the Engineer: The Architecture of Santiago Calatrava*, Artemis: Zurich, 1992

Itsuko Hasegawa, *Itsuko Hasegawa*, Academy Editions: London, 1993

Dean Hawkes, *The Environmental Tradition - Studies in the Architecture of Environment*, E & FN Spon: London, 1996

Thomas Herzog, ed., *Solar Energy in Architecture and Planning*, Prestel: Munich, 1996

John Hix, *The Glasshouse*, second edition, Phaidon: London, 1996

Angus J. MacDonald, *Structure and Architecture*, Architectural Press: Oxford, 1994

Volkwin Marg, *New Trade Fair Leipzig*, Birkhäuser: Berlin, 1996

Rowan Moore, ed., *Structure Space and Skin: The Work of Nicholas Grimshaw and Partners*, Phaidon: London, 1993

Jeremy Myerson, *New Public Architecture*, Laurence King: London, 1996

Frei Otto, Bodo Rasch, *Finding Form*, Edition Axel Menges: Fellbach, 1995

Victor Papanek, *The Green Imperative*, Thames and Hudson: London, 1995

Henry Plummer, *Light in Japanese Architecture*, A+U Publishing: Tokyo, 1995

Kenneth Powell, *Stansted: Norman Foster and the Architecture of Flight*, Fourth Estate and Wordsearch: London, 1992

Peter Rice, *An Engineer Imagines*, Artemis: London, 1994

Peter Rice and Hugh Dutton, *Structural Glass*, E & F N Spon: London, 1995

Terence Riley, *Light Construction*, Publications Department, Museum of Modern Art New York: New York, 1995

Richard Rogers, *Architecture, a Modern View*, Thames and Hudson: London, 1990

Dennis Sharp, ed., *Santiago Calatrava*, E & F N Spon: London, 1994

Michael Spens, ed., *William Alsop and Jan Störmer*, Academy Editions: London, 1993

Deyan Sudjic, *The 100 Mile City*, Andre Deutsch: London, 1992

Deyan Sudjic, *The Architecture of Richard Rogers*, Wordsearch: London, 1994

Benedetta Tagliabue Miralles, ed., *Enric Miralles Works and Projects 1975-1995*: New York, 1996

Maggie Toy, ed., *Visions for the Future*, Academy Group: London, 1993

Maggie Toy, ed., *Tensile Structures*, Academy Group: London, 1995

Brenda and Robert Vale, *Green Architecture - Design for a Sustainable Future*, Thames and Hudson: London, 1996

Michael Wigginton, *Glass in Architecture*, Phaidon: London, 1996

Chris Wilkinson, *Supersheds*, second edition, Butterworth Architecture: Oxford, 1996

Ken Yeang, *The Skyscraper Bioclimatically Considered*, Academy Editions: London, 1996

Laura C. Zeiher, *The Ecology of Architecture*, Whitney Library of Design: New York, 1996